COUPS & CONS

by
Graham Sharpe

Cartoons by Clive Collins

AESCULUS PRESS

DEDICATION

To John Kay for providing the idea and the Silver Springs Hotel, Jersey for providing the location and relaxation for planning it out and reading the proofs!

Cover design by Legend Design Consultants, Bristol.

First Published 1991
by Aesculus Press,
P.O.Box 10, Oswestry,
Shropshire SY10 7QR.

Typeset by Aesculus Press using MICROSOFT WORD
Output on a Hewlett Packard HP Laserjet III.

Printed and bound in Great Britain by
C.G.S. Print Group, Ellesmere Port, S.Wirral, L66 1ST.

1-871093-41-4

ABOUT THE AUTHOR......

Graham Sharpe was born in November, 1950. He started writing for a living in the summer of 1968 when he joined the Middlesex Weekly Post newspaper and has rarely stopped tapping away on a typewriter (he's not into new-fangled word processors) since.

These days, though, he is on the other side of the fence, as it were. Instead of writing for newspapers he spends most of his days dealing with queries from journalists in his position as Media Relations Manager for bookmakers William Hill.

He has to his credit a number of gambling-related books. The first of these, *Racing Ready Reckoner* (Pan), was compiled and written in collaboration with then colleague now Greyhound Manager at Wembley Stadium, Mike Raper.

When this slight but informative tome failed to crack the best seller lists Graham struck out on his own with *Rare Stakes*, published by Pan in 1986.

Concerned lest the punning title of this anecdotal collection of betting yarns should have seen it ending up alongside the other cookery books, Graham was more straightforward next time out - and 1988's *The Sporting Life Book of Amazing Bets* was just that - amazing!

In 1990 Guinness published Graham's first hardback offering, *Turf Accounts*, while he has also contributed chapters to both editions of *The Sporting Life Guide To How To Pick Winners*.

In his private life Graham is married to Sheila, and their seventeen year stint has resulted in two sons - Steeven (spelt that way to aggravate Graham's Mum), now 11; and Paul, now 7.

Graham, still running round on a soccer pitch each Sunday morning for the Veterans branch of the Hatch End Football Club of which he is Manager, has being trying to rid himself of the unfortunate handicap of supporting Luton Town almost ever since acquiring it in 1959. However, having just become a season ticket holder for the first time it seems he is stuck with it - especially as Steeven has now been likewise afflicted. What's more, a dog called Luton Town has been winning regularly at Hackney and at time of writing the Sharpe family fortunes were £13.75 better off as a direct result!

How is Sharpe qualified to write a book on Gambling Coups and Cons?

Well, having been the target of a number of determined conmen during the pursuance of his employment he has a few interesting tales to tell in which he has a direct personal involvement, and he has also made it his business to seek out some of the more notable gambling coups and cons of the recent and distant past.

His own greatest gambling coup came when a well informed 'insider' told him to get on the 'good thing' John Major at 33-1 for the Leadership of the Tory Party, and his greatest con was perpetrated against the representative of a rival bookmaker. The pair of them had been invited on to a radio chat show to discuss political betting. Aware that his rival was there to talk about a brand new bet they had just introduced, Sharpe made sure that he was questioned first by the host, claimed the rival's bet for himself and left the other representative speechless and furious when the time came for his interview!

All's fair in love, war and gambling, says Sharpe - and in this book you'll read precious little about love and war, but plenty about gambling methods fair and foul.

Chapter I

I was certain I was being set up for a con when I received a letter asking me if I'd lay a bet about Oliver Reed's private parts!

The letter was from a (presumably) young lady from Blackpool - to spare her blushes I'll only give her first name, Charmaine.

She wrote: "While reading my Sunday paper, dated 19 Aug 1990, I came across a picture of Ollie Reed exposing his privates to a rather disgusted party of people. It brought back something that a friend told me about a few years ago.

My friend told me he had heard that Ollie Reed had a tattoo on his penis, saying it was something to do with a bird, probably claws or a head or wings, I'm not sure.

I am willing to place a bet, and would be pleased if you would give me odds on the fact, that he does have a tattoo and that it has got something to do with a bird.

I am sure Mr Reed would oblige you with a quick flash as there is no other way of finding out.

PS: I never normally bet - I thought it would be fun to find out the truth as it all sounds pretty painful to me."

I wrote back a cautious letter asking just how much Charmaine had in mind to bet and what we might do if Ollie declined to supply the previously mentioned "quick flash" - but I never heard from her again. She probably thought my reply was a bit below the belt!

∞ ∞ ∞

When a punter who has been betting regularly for thirteen years on the horses suddenly asks you for a price about the Second Coming taking place within a year you begin to wonder whether he may know something you don't!

But the client, a gentleman from Loughborough, was deadly serious and, I hope, 100% genuine - because we struck a bet of £50 at odds of 1000-1 that, within a calendar year, the Archbishop of Canterbury would confirm the Second Coming.

When news of this bet leaked out I received several enquiries from people wishing to have the same bet - including a chap called Mr Stokes from Coventry, who laid out a tenner, and another man from San Francisco who wanted $125.

I must admit to just a small twinge of doubt when David Icke began to make his 'Spirit of the Son of God' comments. A couple of the clients actually rang to claim they had won. One client from Hampstead even claimed HE was the new Messiah!

I even thought I might get the opportunity to check Mr Icke out for myself recently when my son, Steeven, played in a football tournament on the Isle of Wight and discovered the competition he and his team were playing for was the David Icke Trophy.

They reached the Final, and I had high hopes of Mr Icke turning up in person to present the Trophy, so I could see if he wanted a bit of the 1000-1 himself - but in the event he sent his wife.

Still, the good news is that, as yet, there are few signs of the Archbishop paying homage to Mr Icke as the new Messiah, even though the bet increases in popularity: when the papers reported just before the 1991 Wimbledon Tournament that William Hill was offering 1000-1 about either a British player winning the Singles Title, or the Second Coming, the latter was the one which attracted the most cash!

The common perception of a coup is that it involves some element of shady dealing - but it ain't necessarily so; I believe that every punter who places a bet with the expectation of making a profit is planning his or her own coup - albeit a minor one.

And the dictionary backs me up in this theory - my trusty *Collins Modern English* defines the word coup as, "a brilliant and successful stroke or action."

A fine example of a gambling coup would be the World Record winning odds of just over 1,600,000-1, pulled off by George Rhodes of Aldershot. It landed him an £80,000 plus payout for a 5p stake when he picked out seven winners in his accumulative bet.

I was lucky enough to meet George when we took his cheque down to him. "And what will you spend it on, George?" I asked. "Oh, a new Rolls, I should think, the old one's getting on a bit now."

And he wasn't joking.

Born Lucky

I can certainly claim to have been in at 'the birth' of a form of betting which, as yet, has not resulted in a single (or, more accurately, a double) pay-out - even though I was initially apprehensive that I may be letting myself in for the odd sting or two.

The form of betting in question is the placing of wagers about the chances of mothers-to-be giving birth to twins, or triplets.

The nearest anyone has come to conning me was the pregnant lady from Plymouth who backed herself to have a third consecutive set of twins, kept bouncing her cheques until she'd had time to have a scan to make sure she wasn't expecting another pair, and then having the cheek to ask me whether I'd pay her out anyway for having agreed to let me use her name for publicity purposes!

Then there was Newcastle soccer fan Peter Evans, who surprised his wife in the 1990/91 season by backing his side to reach the FA Cup Final at Wembley and his good lady, Linda, to give birth to twins on the same day! Neither event happened.

Or Barbara Cottingham of High Wycombe who made the fairly odd request for odds about her becoming pregnant. It seemed odd because the chances of a woman becoming pregnant at some stage or other surely can't be too great; well, they can if the lady in question has already been sterilised - which Barbara Cottingham has!

She was happy to accept 250-1 against giving birth.

Then there was Vicki D'Arcy, a London lady who was over the moon with the 66-1 I offered about her pregnancy resulting in twins. "That's more than three times better than the odds Ladbrokes offered me," she said delightedly.

"Why bother asking them in the first place?" I wondered.

"I thought I should," she laughed, "after all, I do work for them!"

David Threlfall pulled off one of the best remembered betting coups of all in July 1969 when the 1000-1 odds he'd extracted from William Hill several years earlier about the chances of Man walking on the Moon translated into a £10,000 payout - courtesy of astronaut Neil Armstrong.

Some of the longer surviving members of the William Hill staff still go pale at the memory of how they laughed like drains when first approached by Mr Threlfall about the bet and only offered him the 1000-1 odds to get rid of him.

"If he'd insisted, I think we'd probably have laid him 10,000-1," a relieved staff member confided to me.

That particular coup made it very difficult for anyone looking for a long odds wager to get their money on for some while; "Remember that David Threlfall," came the refrain every time anyone made a slightly out of the ordinary request for a bet.

Take Me To Your Leader

Perhaps inspired by David Threlfall's success, David Greenberg of Blackpool will be £50,000 richer if Man walks on Mars before 1 January 2003. David laid out £1000 at odds of 50-1 with me a couple of years back. To boost his chances of collecting, David has written a novel in which just that happens.

And still up there in space, a gentleman from Bristol, who would prefer to remain anonymous, is expecting to receive the proceeds from his £25 bet at odds of 1000-1 when it is proven that corn circles are formed on fields by the influence of Phobos, one of the moons of Mars.

Aliens from outer space were the subject of a wager struck with me by a certain Mr A. Cockayne of Derby, who stood to win one million pounds if President George Bush should announce that he had come face to face with an extra-terrestrial visitor.

Having placed his bet, Mr Cockayne then wrote to me in January 1990 asking for payment of his winnings.

"I think I've probably won my bet," he confided. "Could you interview the President and confidentially pay the bet if they can't or won't tell the world?"

Nice try, Mr Cockayne!

Credit When It Is Due

I suppose I can claim some of the 'credit' for enabling punters to rekindle their hopes of landing a long-odds coup via a non-racing bet, having specialised in this type of wager for a decade now.

Which is why Robin Davison-Lungley of London is busy persuading his toddler son that he'd prefer to bite on a tennis racket than a dummy - Robin will win a million quid from William Hill on the day that son James becomes the next British winner of the Men's Singles at Wimbledon, having been laid a £100 bet at odds of 10,000-1 against that eventuality, in July 1991.

£1 million is the same sum I'll happily hand over to 'Screaming Lord' David Sutch come the day the British electorate finally vote him in as Prime Minister - he's got £10 at 100,000-1.

£250,000 will be winging its way to Gerald Thomas of Aberdeen when the cheers have died down for his daughter Maloa's achievement of winning an Olympic medal. What do you mean, you've never heard of an athlete called Maloa Thomas? Well, what do you expect, she was only born in 1987, so she's got some way to go yet before winning her call-up to the Olympic squad - but Dad already has £250 on her at 1000-1 to get that Medal.

Oh, and he's got two strings to his bow - Maloa is qualified to represent both Britain and Mexico!

Mr E. Lewis of Pontefract will win £100,000 when his daughter Susan (who will then be 17) wins an Olympic sprint medal in 1996 - for a £20 wager at 5000-1!

Similarly confident in the athletic ability of his off-spring is Richard Stead of Thirsk. His son Charles, who was born in 1972, is already a decent distance runner. Richard is looking for Charles to storm to victory in the London Marathon of the year 2000.

If he does I will be putting a cheque in the post to him for £150,000, after he staked £50 at 3000-1.

Alexander Johnston of Edinburgh has until his 25th birthday in the year 2013 to win £50,000 for his father, by skippering the Scotland soccer team.

Then there are the two ladies from Hereford who have opted for an even more unlikely way of collecting their 5000-1 bet - all they need for a bumper payout is for Elvis Presley to turn up alive!

Scotsman Lenny Blackburn invested £600 on this same bet.

Many of these types of bets have lengthy time limits attached to them, although June Garrett of Stockport was happy enough with the

1995 limit I put on her 100-1 bet that tennis stars Steffi Graf and Boris Becker would wed each other!

Mr H. Blechman of Christchurch, Dorset, is quite content to sit and wait for the year 2031 to come around in order that his particular 1000-1 bet comes up. Antique dealer Mr Blechman will win £20,000 if he is around then to celebrate his own 100th birthday!

I look forward to being invited to the party, especially as I will be the small matter of 81 years old myself, by then - and Mr Blechman will be old enough to put himself up for sale in his antique shop!

This type of bet has become more popular in recent years. It started with a charming old chap, James Hawkins from Dover, who made the first bet of his life at the age of 85 that he'd survive to celebrate his centenary.

So confident was James that he even booked me into a hotel in Dover for a stop-over when I came down with his cheque.

Sadly, James died in 1991, but I was touched to be contacted by one of his daughters who told me what great fun he'd had out of the bet and the publicity that it attracted.

Alan Bishop of Cambridge has been looking to bring off a coup for many years now - he hasn't quite managed it yet, despite having probably the most varied portfolio of bets I've dealt with.

Alan has spent his money (almost always a stake of £12.50 for some reason) wagering that Francis Drake's coffin will be exhumed from the sea; that long lost mountaineers Mallory and Irvine will be discovered in the Himalayas after disappearing there some sixty years ago; that Prince Charles will visit Antarctica; that The Mousetrap will close - and many, many more.

Dr David Wright started a whole new trend when he landed a nice touch by backing his son Andrew to pass 11 GCSE exams with 'A' grades. Having taken a form line from Andrew's head teacher, I offered Dr Wright of Darlington 50-1 to his £20 stake.

I suspected I'd be paying out when the Head Teacher contacted me to ask whether he could have £20 on for himself!

Andrew duly passed all the exams with the necessary 'A' grades.

I hope this lengthy preamble has put you in the right frame of mind for the rest of the book, which consists of a collection of anecdotes and stories about gambling coups and cons, large and small, evil and benign, successful and unsuccessful.

It is not for me to sit in judgment on those who perpetrate such scams, other than to say it is usually a bookie who is at the sharp end of a coup or con - expected to pay up with good grace if caught out, accused of sour grapes if taking any necessary defensive action.

Some of the stories will make you laugh, others will make you wonder at the ingenuity or bare-faced cheek of those involved.

All of them, I trust, will entertain and inform and none of them, I can but pray, will make you want to rush out and rip off your local bookie!

Chapter II

Photo Finished

Bookies at Ayr racecourse became suspicious in the summer of 1990 when two punters kept betting on the outcome of photo-finishes, and proved so successful that they were several thousand pounds up.

A close watch was kept on the men - who were eventually discovered to have rigged up their own video camera system, to film the photo finishes themselves.

They were ejected from the course, but police later dropped charges against the men.

Stroke Of Luck

Investigator Alfredo Lim was appointed by President Cory Aquino to look into alleged rigging in the government-run Philipine National Lottery.

It was apparently pure coincidence that Lim won over £100,000 in the next draw, in July 1990.

Nasty Blow

Alcide, trained by Captain (later Sir) Cecil Boyd-Rochfort, had swept all before him in his preparatory races and was heavily backed to win the 1958 Derby.

In the Lingfield Derby Trial, his final race before Epsom, he pulverised his opponents, winning by 12 lengths.

Eight days later Alcide was found in his box, in agony. In his book *No Secret So Close* Bruce Hobbs, assistant trainer to the Captain at the time, wrote:

"There was a large lump or swelling on his near-side back ribs. There is no doubt that he had been 'got at' and had been given a vicious blow which had probably broken a rib. He had to be scratched from the Derby, won by the Irish outsider Hard Ridden, who was clearly not in the same class as Alcide."

Once again the nobblers had succeeded.

Hobbs is also convinced the Queen's Mulberry Harbour was doped before the Oaks of 1957, from which she returned, "absolutely staggering, with her eyes glazed."

Nearly A Grand Idea

On 30 June 1964, a gang of punters launched one of the most ingenious attempted gambling cons of all - The Dagenham Dog Coup.

The 4.05 race over 840 yards included three fancied dogs and three complete no-hopers. The plan was that the riggers would place just one bet covering all possible first-second combinations of the three fancied dogs on the course tote machine, before placing a vast number of combination bets on the no-hopers.

This would mean that if the race went to plan a huge dividend would be returned on the winning forecast combination - and the gang would have placed a large number of off-course bets on the three fancied dogs to cash in.

To ensure the plan worked, the gang worked out a system; as soon as the previous race was run, their members would move in to every tote window and prevent any members of the general public from placing bets.

It all went like clockwork, and bets were placed off-course in some 400 betting shops by an estimated 100 men, who stood to collect up to £10 million.

The second favourite, Buckwheat, won the race, ahead of third favourite, Handsome Lass.

The syndicate had staked 11,757 units on the Tote - with only one unit naming the correct winning forecast (traps 5 and 1).

The returned dividend was an amazing £987 11s 9d!

All hell broke loose - and the bookies refused to pay.

Despite court cases lasting two years, no-one was ever paid. Stake money was refunded.

Romford based punter John Turner, allegedly the ring-leader, was prosecuted for fraud - but he and the others were eventually awarded costs. However, they had been so greedy there was never any prospect that they would be paid.

Sleight Of Hand

The 10-1 shot which won the Knighton Auction Stakes for two-year-olds at Leicester in March 1982 was listed on the racecard as Flockton Grey.

But it was another horse, Good Hand, which had run under Flockton Grey's name. The winning distance of 20 lengths was unsurprising - Good Hand was, in fact, a three-year-old!

It was alleged in court that racehorse owner Kenneth Richardson had, together with two accomplices, netted £36,000 by backing Flockton Grey/Good Hand.

He was charged with conspiracy to defraud bookmakers by switching the horses and eventually received a nine month sentence, suspended for a year, plus a fine of £20,000 and £100,000 costs.

Sounds Suspicious

Riding Ile De Chypre, who had been backed from 6-1 to 4-1 second favourite, in the King George V Handicap at Royal Ascot, Greville Starkey had taken the horse into a clear lead when, in the words of the respected *Ruffs Guide To The Turf*, the horse, "swerved badly left and unseated the rider inside the final furlong."

For over a year the incident remained a mystery until, in October 1989, a certain James Laming went on trial in a case involving a multi-million pound cocaine chain.

Suddenly, during the trial, Laming claimed that he and another man had devised a system to undermine the fabric of racecourse betting.

As if this wasn't fantastic enough on its own, Laming then declared he had invented a set of binoculars capable of emitting sound-waves which were inaudible to humans, but when aimed at a horse could cause it to swerve, stop or start in an erratic manner.

Laming further claimed that these binoculars had been used on Ile De Chypre, in order to land a gambling coup.

Controversy raged as to whether this 'stun-gun' tale was plausible or merely a smokescreen to deflect attention from the real point of the trial.

Greville Starkey took part in re-enactments of the Ile De Chypre situation, and some respected judges announced their belief in the 'stun-gun' theory - although no concrete proof ever emerged. Laming was convicted of the cocaine related offences.

Personally, I very much doubt the veracity of the stun-gun 'coup' scenario - no unusual betting patterns associated with the race were ever noticed and it wasn't as if this particular horse was a hot favourite. Of course, it could be argued that the Ile de Chypre episode was a trial run - imagine the security implications of having to check out every set of binoculars taken on to a racecourse if this scam were ever proved feasible!

Bright Spark

One of the most recent, and most blatant, ringer affairs concerned a small meeting at Rochester, Victoria (Australia), in November 1987, when Spark Plug finished last in a heat for a Cup event (one with a heat/final format). Spark Plug later took the place of another horse, Tom, which had qualified for the final, only to be injured.

Spark Plug duly ran as 'Tom' and won the race. The Stewards, though, discovered the switch and disqualified him - whereupon the owner/trainer of Spark Plug wrote to the Stewards expressing his opinion that as the horse had run and won he should still receive the prize money and Cup!

Hold-up

In 1984, some unscrupulous punters discovered a way of tapping in to the commentaries being broadcast into south coast betting shops. They then delayed the relaying of the greyhound racing commentaries by some thirty seconds - giving themselves time to discover which dog had won the race and still get accomplices to place bets before the race was apparently even under way.

Wise After The Event

American gambling expert John Scarne, author of numerous books on the subject, told how he unravelled one of the most ingenious scams he'd ever come across. It was pulled in the sixties by a group of women called the Blondie Mob, operating at the time when racing results were only released from the track to the outside world after the last race had been run.

The Mob was operating in Hollywood and Scarne was called in when a bookmaker, who had lost $100,000 to a woman in just four weeks, became suspicious. The bookie operated from a room on the top floor of a building, and told Scarne:

"It's air conditioned, soundproof and has no windows. What's more, my players must arrive here before post time (the 'off' of races). After post time, no-one is allowed off the elevator at this floor until after the last race. The bettors are not permitted to make or receive phone calls while they are here, and the phone number is not listed."

Scarne spent an afternoon watching Blondie at work. "I could see at once she didn't have a radio-receiving gimmick on her; the low necked dress she wore was a tight fit and no room to spare."

By the end of the afternoon she had won $2000 - but Scarne was on to her. He told the bookie: "She's been past-posting you, and the guy who has been tipping her off is you! "

Scarne revealed that Blondie's confederate must be whoever had phoned through a bet on Snow Shoes in the eighth race at Hialeah.

"That was May - another blonde," said the bookie.

Explained Scarne: "May is operating from a room that has a direct line from one of the wire services. She gets the result of the race a minute after it's over. As soon as she knew High Noon had won the third race she phoned and gave you a bet of 50, 20 and 10 on Snow Shoes in the 8th and asked you to repeat it, which you did. Blondie heard you say, 'You bet me 50, 20 and 10 on Snow Shoes in the 8th at Hialeah' and simply added the first digits of the amount of the bet, got an answer of 8 and knew that the horse listed as number 8 on her scratch sheet had won the 3rd race."

See No Evil...

One of the most dramatic illustrations of the potential of dope was carried out just after the turn of the century by trainer George Lambton, who was worried that the Stewards of the Jockey Club were turning a blind eye to the increasingly widespread use of dope.

Lambton told the Stewards he intended to dope six of his own horses which had shown little ability in the past. Four of them immediately won races, one was second and the other wasn't actually given anything.

This finally convinced the racing hierarchy, who then made a warning-off the punishment for the use of dope.

Leg-Pulls

Australian jockey Ted Webster took drastic measures when he felt that fellow jockey J.Meagher, riding Iskander, was getting the better of matters in a handicap race at Moonee Valley, Melbourne, in 1933.

Webster, on board Blematic, grabbed at the tail of Iskander, and when that failed to slow the horse and jockey down, he grabbed hold of Meagher's leg to hold him back!

Unfortunately for Webster, Iskander still managed to win the race but the leg-pulling jockey found himself disqualified for twelve months.

Twenty eight years later, in the 1961 AJC Derby, Queensland jockey Mel Schumacher, riding Blue Era, grabbed hold of jockey Tom Hill's knee to prevent him and his mount Summer Fair crossing the line first.

The ploy was initially successful - Blue Era prevailing by half a head - only for the result to be reversed and Schumacher warned off for life, a sentence later reduced to five and a half years.

In 1942 Adelaide jockey K.Parris was disqualified for six months after being found guilty of hanging onto the tail of a rival horse - just as it was about to jump a fence in a steeplechase!

Dubious Claim

Spoon bending is a pretty amazing ability claimed by Uri Geller - but another feat he claims must be regarded as even more unlikely.

In his autobiography the Israeli showman claims he used his psychic powers to win £17,000 from a London Casino. That would be amazing enough, but Geller then goes on to claim he felt so guilty at exploiting his gift in this way that to salve his conscience he threw away all the money out of his car window.

Not So Wise Owls

On 12 April 1964, *The People* carried a story headlined 'The Biggest Sports Scandal Of The Century', which named three First Division footballers, two of them international players, as having been involved in the 'fixing' of a match - each of them having had a bet of £50 which included their own side being beaten.

They were David 'Bronco' Layne, Peter Swan and Tony Kay, and all three had played for Sheffield Wednesday in a 2-0 defeat at Ipswich on 1 Dec 1962. They each made £100 profit on their bets.

The story was the culmination of investigations which had been continuing since 1960, when Stoke goalkeeper Jimmy O'Neill had reported being approached to throw a match against Norwich. The key man in the story turned out to be Jimmy Gauld, a Scottish soccer player who had suffered a broken leg whilst playing for Mansfield Town. He had apparently set up a network of players being paid to rig games which he then bet on. In 1964, he claimed his syndicate was netting £1000 a week by betting on Fixed Odds coupons.

The Sheffield Wednesday trio and several other lesser known players were duly charged, along with Gauld.

Layne, Swan and Kay were each given four months imprisonment and were banned from soccer for life - Swan and Layne subsequently had their bans lifted and they played again in 1972, but Kay emigrated to Spain and had no further involvement with the game, although in mid 1991 he turned out in midfield for a Pro-Celebrity side including a number of former internationals and 'soap' stars against whom I was playing for a team representing a local school. It was a charity match so although we were losing at half-time I resisted the temptation of offering Kay a fiver to 'go easy' in the second half!

Gauld was sent to jail for four years and ordered to pay £5000 costs.

During the course of its investigations, The People turned up a number of matches strongly believed to have been fixed. Most notably, on 7 April 1963, it reported about bookies who had paid out £100,000 to punters who had taken 6-4 about a Derby-Stockport double. The two sides had duly obliged, winning 6-2 and 4-1.

Shock Results

In October 1961, two sides who had previously won just one away match that season, played sides with good home records and were heavily backed in a 10-1 double - they were Tranmere, who won at York, and Bradford City, who won at Mansfield.

After investigations, the bookmakers refused to pay up and claimed to have identified twelve punters placing large numbers of bets on the double. The only one who insisted on pursuing a claim once the rigging allegations had been made was a certain Jimmy Gauld.

Should Have Woon

In 1990, Malaysian newspapers reported that a jockey called K.C.Woon had been disqualified for five years, after the Stewards decided he had deliberately jumped off a horse called Joy Of The Jungle during a race at Penang, in which he was leading with a furlong to run.

Illegal Bookmakers

Legal bookmakers estimates of the amount of illegal gambling which takes place in the country are often rubbished by those who believe they are 'talking up' the problem for political reasons - but some idea of the genuine scale of the problem nationwide can be gathered from a report which appeared in *The Independent*, and elsewhere, in April 1991.

Workers at Rover's Longbridge car factory in Birmingham bet a staggering £132,000 with an illegal shop floor bookmaking business that made nearly £40,000 profit, revealed the paper.

Bromsgrove magistrates were told that two men admitted nine charges of evading betting duty and one charge of failing to notify Customs and Excise of their business. The two men were said to have accepted up to 100 bets a day with the help of specially recruited runners from different parts of the factory.

The men, who worked on different shifts, met at lunchtime outside a factory gate to update their records, which they kept in exercise books bought from Woolworths!

They made some £40,000 on the venture, but failed to collect more than £10,000 in betting duty. The two were each ordered to do 200 hours community service and fined £750 with £150 costs!

Illegal gambling is a genuine problem - I know of cases where illegal bookies have literally set up their own betting shop within a betting shop, intercepting genuine punters on their way to the counter to place a bet and offering to lay them the bet without any deductions.

This is all well and good as long as the punter is backing losers or small money winners - but let him land a long-priced accumulator and then try to find the bookie to pay him out!

Tom Kelly, Director General of BOLA, the Betting Office Licensees Association, is another man very concerned with the scale of illegal gambling and he commented on the Longbridge case: "If this is the level of penalty we can expect the courts to impose then betting duty offences will thrive. In 1982 we carried out an exhaustive investigation and concluded that the turnover on illegal betting was equal to 15 to 20 per cent of turnover on legal betting. There is no reason to believe this has changed."

In 1989, Customs and Excise gaming teams took 147 people to court, of whom six were imprisoned. Fines totalling more than

£100,000 were levied by courts.

Betting shops today are an accepted part of the High Street scene - reputable, well run and completely legitimate.

In 1847, Messrs Drummond and Greville opened the first betting shop in London. Within three years there were four hundred, most of them rather suspect - as contemporary reports confirm.

"Many of the smaller betting shops were simply traps for the unwary. The stock in trade needed was merely a few fly-blown racing prints and some old ledgers. A room was soon hired, often in some derelict tobacconist's shop, and business then commenced. Most of these places existed in obscure and dirty thoroughfares; the neighbourhood of Drury Lane being especially affected by those indulging in this nefarious industry.

Just before a big race meeting, such as the Derby or Ascot, numbers of these betting shops would burst into bloom for a short space of time. When the meetings ended, the crowd coming to get paid would find the proprietor gone and the place in charge of a boy, who, generally not at all disconcerted, would announce that his master had gone out on 'tickler bizness' and would not be back till late at night. His wife also had gone out of town for her health 'till the winter'. 'Will he be back tomorrow?' would cry the crowd. 'No he won't be here tomorrow 'cos it's Sunday and he always goes to church on Sunday'. The crowd would, for the time being, reluctantly disperse, to return again time after time with the same ill success, till eventually, realising that they had been duped, the bell-pull was torn out and the windows broken, the proprietor meanwhile doing a flourishing business in some other locality."

Another report declared: "A man named Dwyer, who kept a cigar shop and betting house in St Martin's Lane in 1851, was in the habit of laying a point or two more than the regular odds, and in consequence did the largest business of any list man in London. He was considered to be absolutely safe. It was the custom to pay the day following a big race, but when Miss Nancy won the Chester Cup, his doors were found to be closed and the house being broken into by an enormous crowd of infuriated creditors, everything valuable was discovered to have been removed. Dwyer, as a matter of fact, had bolted with about £25,000 of the public's money."

This incident sparked a huge outcry and in July 1853 an Act entitled 'An Act for the Suppression of Betting Houses' was passed which, "inflicted on anyone keeping or assisting to keep any house, office, room or place for the purpose of betting, a penalty not exceeding one hundred pounds, or imprisonment with or without hard labour for any time not exceeding six calendar months."

It was not until 1 May 1961 that betting shops became legal again.

Money Back Bottle

Golfer Lee Trevino used to con opponents by offering to play against them using a soft drinks bottle instead of a golf club. Little did they know he had practised for a year with the bottle.

Trevino revealed in his autobiography: "I played with that bottle for three years against all-comers and never lost."

His Number Came Up

In 1930, a Cincinnati clearinghouse clerk was bribed to rig the last three digits of the daily balance for 11 December, so that they read 000.

These would be the winning digits in the illegal 'numbers' game played in New York, where there were currently over 1000 'banks' or numbers operators.

The people who bribed the clerk set about betting on the winning group of numbers, staking around $10,000. The numbers came up at odds of 600-1. The banks owed $6,000,000. Hundreds of them were forced to close or default. The plotters probably only collected a tenth of what they stood to win.

The episode ended with several murders - and the disappearance of the clearinghouse clerk.

Jumbo Size

In 1961, Pinturischio was hot favourite for the Derby. A month before the race a gang broke into Noel Murless's stable, found their way into the horse's box by picking a lock and gave him a powerful physic usually used for elephants.

Pinturischio became so ill that he never ran again.

£250,000 of ante-post bets were believed to have been lost.

A Dog's Life

Beau Brummel, whose sense of fashion means he is still famous today, once conned his way to victory over a bet.

Enjoying an afternoon's shooting, he had taken on a wager with his host for a substantial sum that he would take the heaviest bag of anyone on the shoot.

The host accepted, and was doing rather better than Beau as the day drew to a close.

Nothing if not resourceful, Beau took a rather desperate measure to ensure his bag was indeed heavier than anyone else's - he shot the host's pointer bitch.

The Oldest One In The Book

'Find the Lady' and 'Thimble and Pea' cons are commonplace at racecourses, circuses and fairgrounds even today, but in an 1829 book *The Turf Expositor*, C.F.Brown describes a con which has

changed little over the years:

"A fellow lounges about with a small table, followed at a short distance by a confederate or two. When he perceives a likely customer, down goes the table, upon which he places three large thimbles. He covers the pea with one (or seems to cover it), moves the thimble to and fro, and offers to bet from 'one to ten sovereigns' that the byestander cannot tell which thimble covers the pea: his confederates advance and play; they win and thus it is endeavoured to draw the byestander into the snare.

If we consider this infamous robbery of the unwary, it will be immediately perceived that the odds are 2 to 1 in favour of the table at first glance; but the fact is, there is no chance for the player; these fellows have a dexterous method of either removing the pea altogether, or placing it under one of the thimbles, as it may happen to suit their purpose, and thus to make sure of their prey."

Indeed, in Doncaster in 1829 the 'Thimblemen' had become such a problem that the local townspeople called up special constabulary and Yeomanry to put them to flight. A contemporary report described what happened: "Hundreds of ruffians carrying bludgeons, often the stout legs of their thimble tables, prepared to resist, but, in pitched and brutal battle they were routed and their ringleaders arrested."

Home Banker?

Former Celtic, Manchester United and Scotland midfield player Lou Macari found himself in the midst of a furore over a £6500 bet on the team he managed being beaten.

Macari was manager of Second Division Swindon Town when the bet was struck on his team to be beaten in an away FA Cup tie at Newcastle in January 1988.

Newcastle were 8-13 favourites and won the match 5-0, leaving a £4000 profit on the £6500 stake.

There was no suggestion at all that the match had been fixed, but following a hearing in February 1990, Macari - by then manager of West Ham - and Brian Hillier, the Swindon Chairman, were found guilty by the Football Association of breaching their rule regarding betting on matches.

Macari was fined £1000 and censured, while Hillier was suspended from taking an active role in the game for six months. Swindon were fined £7500.

The rule breached was rule 26a (iv) which states that a member shall be found guilty of misconduct if they are found guilty of "betting on any football match other than on authorised and registered Football Pools".

In A State

A big poker showdown took place in 1889 at Bowen's Saloon,

Santa Fe, New Mexico, where cattle baron Ike Baron and professional gambler Johnny Dougherty faced each other over the table.

The Governor, L.Bradford Prince, and almost 100 prominent local VIPs were in attendance for this much vaunted confrontation.

With $100,000 in the pot Jackson ran out of cash, but wrote out a deed to his ranch to raise Dougherty.

The fast thinking pro demanded writing materials and scribbled on a piece of paper - handing it to the Governor at the same time as he whipped out his gun and demanded: "Governor, sign this, or you're dead."

The Governor signed, Dougherty threw the piece of paper into the pot and said: "I'm raising you the Territory of New Mexico. There's the deed."

Jackson threw in his hand.

Hitting The Jackpot

A 21-year-old man from York claimed he was winning up to £1000 per week from fruit machines - but gave up playing the machines because spending up to eighteen hours a day playing them was ruining his eyesight.

The former labourer's story emerged in The Sun in June 1991, and the newspaper put him to the test to prove his abilities. They reported: "We watched him pocket £50 in 45 minutes with a stake of £5."

Kevin Cooper said that his success was based on having super-fast reflexes and being able to memorise many of the sequences of the machines.

His success had caused him to be banned from dozens of pubs, arcades and motorway service stations where he would play the machines.

"A lot of people would like a job like mine," said Cooper, "but it's dreadful - I often fear I am going to get mugged when I leave a pub with my pockets bulging with £1 coins and 50p pieces. I'm getting short-sighted from staring for hours on end at the reels and flashing lights."

Announcing that he intended to give up his career, Cooper said: "I bet a lot of landlords and arcade owners will be breathing a heavy sigh of relief - some have been very unhappy when they see how much I've been winning. But what I do is completely legal."

Key Witness

In 1834, 5-6 St Leger favourite Plenipotentiary finished 10th of 11 runners, and was widely believed to have been got at. Many years later his travelling head lad confessed he had been bribed to lend the key to the horse's box for an hour.

Striking Gold

When a woman gambler turned £100 into £750,000 during the course of one session at London's Golden Horseshoe Casino, in 1991, security staff became suspicious.

After the woman had left, clutching her winnings in cheques, they took the roulette wheel on which she had been gambling apart and examined it thoroughly.

The very next day the Casino put a stop on all the woman's winning cheques and called in police and Gaming Board officials.

Reported the *London Evening Standard* on 20 June 1991: "Something 'unnatural' had happened to the wheel," said a spokesman. "There was something wrong with the wheel and we couldn't stop the game while it was in progress. We examined it afterwards and the internal security people found there would appear to have been something unnaturally wrong with it."

Commented a Casino Director: "Our own security staff and management acted very promptly and efficiently to avoid a major loss."

Scotland Yard Regional Crime Squad detectives were called in to investigate the matter.

No Doubts

Few punters actually welcome backing a loser, but one hopes even fewer would be prepared to go to the lengths of murdering their bookmaker in order not to have to settle up.

But that is how far a certain William Palmer was prepared to go in 1853 when he had £500 riding on the chances of his 7-1 shot, Doubt, which he fully expected to win the Wolverhampton Handicap.

Palmer - a surgeon by profession - was a character of dubious morals. He had already been strongly suspected of fatally poisoning two other people to whom he owed gambling debts, yet he was nevertheless popular on the racecourse.

On this occasion he was travelling to the races with Frederick Swindell, one of the biggest and most reputable bookmakers of the day, who had already reportedly told a fellow bookie, George Hodgman, of the trip.

Hodgman had warned Swindell of Palmer's reputation but Swindell had replied: "I shall be alright. Bye the bye, Palmer says he has a good thing in Doubt for the handicap. I've put him £500 on at sevens, and I've got £250 on myself."

The key point here was that Palmer had somehow persuaded Swindell to stake the £500 bet for him in his own name. If Swindell were to expire before settling day in the event of Doubt losing, the bet would be void.

Palmer and Swindell enjoyed a drink together the evening before race day. Palmer persuaded Swindell to drink so much brandy - almost certainly liberally laced with other deadly liquids - that he was too ill to attend the races the next day. If Doubt lost, Palmer clearly planned to return to Swindell and to finish him off by administering more poison.

Fortunately for Swindell the horse, literally running for life, prevailed by half a length. Now Palmer returned to Swindell to apply the antidote to the poison and the bookmaker duly recovered and was able to pay Palmer his winnings.

However, Palmer went from bad to worse - poisoning his wife after taking out a £14,000 insurance policy on her and then doing likewise to his brother! He was finally tried and convicted in 1856 of murdering another turf acquaintance, John Parsons Cook, a crime for which he was hanged.

Enclosure Disclosure

Chief In Charge was really buzzing at Balmoral Park, Chicago in December 1990 - and so, to the disgust of those punters in the know who forced the horse's odds down from 50-1 to 7-1, was his jockey!

For, after Chief In Charge stormed to victory, racecourse security officials spotted jockey Geary E.Louviere discarding an electrical 'buzzer' device and promptly voided the race. The device would be used to administer a stimulating jolt or charge to the horse, spurring it on to greater effort.

Said Balmoral Vice President John Johnson: "In the winners circle the security guard said, 'You're coming with us'. Louviere said, 'I'll be right with you'. He then turned his back and undid his trousers and the device fell out.

A security guard picked it up immediately. It was a buzzer, an illegal electrical apparatus used to stimulate a horse."

On The Fiddle

Cunning old card sharp James Ashby enlisted the services of a young accomplice to outwit the gamblers who saw them as an easy touch on the Mississippi riverboats in the early nineteenth century.

The young accomplice would masquerade as a wealthy young buck just waiting to be fleeced, while Ashby would play a bumbling old fool who staggered around playing the fiddle.

It was only much later, after they'd lost their cash, that the gamblers who made a beeline for the youngster learned that Ashby was signalling to him by means of the tunes he played on the fiddle, telling him just which cards to play and when.

Chapter III

On To A Winner

The mythical searches for the Holy Grail, the secret of eternal life and the mystery of the alchemist's art are as nothing compared with the frantic cravings of the average punter to discover the perfect betting system.

The system doesn't exist - at least, not legally. But back in 1982, a Cornish gentleman, who called himself Mr Winner, decided that it did, and what was more, he also believed he'd discovered it.

What to do with this system, thought Mr Winner. "I know, I'll blackmail the bookies with it - and I'll start with that Graham Sharpe at William Hill." So he duly wrote to me - demanding a cool half a million pounds - otherwise he would unleash his system upon my company!

Wrote Mr Winner: "I have always believed that there was a system that would work. During the holidays last year I came up with what I considered to be a foolproof system. I watched the results every day, and every day my system worked and showed an average profit of £2000 each week. At present I am the only person who knows it. When I realised the full potential of it I decided to offer it to you, thinking that you would want to buy it so that you could take out a world copyright on it. This would mean that I could not sell it to any other punters. My price for this system is £500,000."

Mr Winner was a thoughtful chap, though:

"I obviously do not expect you to send a cheque for £500,000 through the post. When you have made your decision please send your reply to the address shown on my SAE. If you do not pay I promise that I will not only use it myself, but I will tell it to a few mates and move around the country and win that money within five years."

I replied to Mr Winner, inviting him to go ahead and set about bankrupting us with his system.

Shortly after he rang to tell me: "Last week we 'ad £560, all right?" Believing that William Hill could just about sustain this level of losses for a week or two I didn't panic.

Then Mr Winner wrote again: "I did as you suggested. In the week ending 17.4.82 my total profit - excluding petrol - was £875.50. As you can see I am very serious about this matter of getting my deserved £500,000."

Declaring that he was now thinking of advertising the system, Mr Winner continued: "If your bosses are daft enough to say no without even seeing me face to face then say so as it will save me wondering whether to order my new Lotus now, as there is a twenty week waiting list, or leave it until the money comes pouring in from my advert. Do not forget that it is cheaper for you to pay me for my system than to be made bankrupt."

And with that he was gone - never to be heard of again - and for all I know he may now be living it up on a tropical island with enough money to burn.

Then again, he may not.

∞ ∞ ∞

As if the threat of Mr Winner wasn't enough to deal with, I then received some correspondence from a Mr Porter of Somerset, once again willing, for a small consideration no doubt, to save us from ruin by divulging the details of his infallible system to me.

"Oh Mr Porter, what shall I do?" I felt like singing as I read his letter telling me, "I am now in a position to sell the information I have. Obviously I am not willing to divulge this without coming to some agreement with either yourselves or any other interested person.

We can prove without doubt that we can beat bookmakers on the course. We have been successful at the four courses we have visited - Bath, Chepstow, Salisbury and Windsor. There is no risk whatsoever. I have discussed the matter with a solicitor friend and he implied, without a change in the racing rules, he felt it to be quite legal."

I wondered to myself whether the 'solicitor friend' had also advised Mr Porter about the legality of threatening bookmakers, but read on.

"To recap, we can, without the risk of loss to ourselves, bet on different races at most racecourses and win money - we have calculated on average, if we were to go daily, between two and three thousand pounds a week."

At this point I was wondering if they'd let me team up with them - but dismissed such unworthy thoughts and struggled on.

"I guarantee, if I divulge this information to you it could be stopped overnight. If the racing authorities are not interested I will sell this through the media to the general public. We have proved it works, it's just now a matter of ethics." Ethics? I thought he was from Thomerthet!

Needless to say, Mr Porter was advised that as the company's Blackmail Budget had been exhausted for the time being, he'd better get on and bankrupt us and every other bookie in the kingdom by using his system.

Perhaps he's out there now at Bath, Chepstow, Salisbury or Windsor, putting it into practice.

Or, again, perhaps not.

Tennis Racket

Mr Winner was possibly the first, but definitely not the last, punter to endeavour to defraud William Hill out of some substantial sums.

Ian Moo Young contacted me in 1988, telling me he fancied his chances of winning Wimbledon in 1989. Not that he had too many immediate obvious qualifications for so doing.

He was 45 years old, born in Jamaica of Chinese parents, and living in England where he ran a successful business making films for advertising commercials.

He'd been playing tennis for less than a month, but such was his confidence in his own abilities that he would gladly stake money on the likelihood of everything from reaching the qualifying rounds of Wimbledon to actually winning the Tournament.

After a couple of meetings with him, during which time he impressed me with his business sense and his sense of eccentricity, we agreed a sliding scale of bets which ended at odds of 50,000-1 for him to win Wimbledon - he staked £20 on this, which would net him £1 million, along with a string of lesser bets.

We agreed we would launch him and his bets on the world's press as the Briton who was finally going to win Wimbledon.

We hired the prestigious Queens Club and tried to find a suitable opponent to take him on in his first ever public game. The top two British tennis players declined after we refused to reveal the identity of the player they would face, even though we assured them he would be British.

Finally, the then British number five, Nick Brown, agreed to take on Moo (as he liked to be known) in a demo game.

The press conference launching Moo went off well - until he went a little over the top by announcing he would win Wimbledon using only the side of his racquet rather than the strings!

He duly failed to qualify for the tournament and that seemed to be that, until journalists began to ring me up asking me whether we intended to stand by our bets with Moo.

"Why shouldn't we? " I asked - whereupon they explained that Moo had now contacted the media, claiming he had actually backed himself not to win the Wimbledon tournament at the All England Club, but the WIMBLEDON CLUB tournament - quite a different affair - entered by only a dozen or so club players at a tennis club over the road from the world famous lawns!

TV, radio and newspapers became very interested in Moo who had, in fact, managed to place a large number of bets with other bookmakers that he would win this other tournament, all of which had been accepted in the assumption that Moo was talking about the real thing.

A campaign was launched on behalf of Moo by one particularly aggressive TV programme - but I was finally able to scupper his claims for payment by the simple expedient of ringing up the other

Wimbledon club to check on Moo's progress in their tournament. I discovered he had failed to get past the second round. Phew!

'Silly Moo' aces the bookies

SERVICE WITH A SMILE: Player Moo-Young with one of his bets   Picture: STEVE BENT

By SARAH POLAND

ONCE they called him 'Silly Moo,' but yesterday tennis player Ian Moo-Young revealed himself as anything but daft.

The unknown amateur player, who has backed himself to win up to £3 million if he triumphs at Wimbledon, is about to serve the bookies an ace.

When Moo-Young wagered £2,000 at odds of up to 500-to-1, bookies fell over themselves to take his money — without, he claims, looking at the small print.

His 66 betting slips clearly state they refer to the Wimbledon Club Tournament, a small-time amateur competition played for laughs across the road from the famous All England Tennis and Croquet Club.

Moo-Young's bet made headlines when it was announced last November.

But now the 45-year-old film maker reveals: 'I didn't mean THE Wimbledon.

'My betting slips make it clear I'm betting on

Last November's headlines

myself to win the Wimbledon Club Tournament later this month, not the big event.

'Corals are trying to get out of it and have been asking for their betting slips back. I think you can say they are worried, but it is all here in black and white so there can be no arguments.'

Moo-Young, a Briton born in Jamaica of Chinese parents, has been working on his game.

And he has been taking expert advice from professionals Tim Wilkinson and Sergio Casal.

He won a small club tournament — the Rookfield Tennistar Invitation — in London last month,

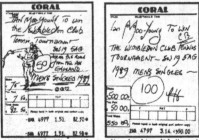

SURE BETS: Slips with wording bookies didn't spot

and says he backed himself to win £1,000. He said: 'The sparks will fly. I have what you might call a powerful incentive to win. Get your money on.'

A spokesman for Corals said he could not say anything about the bet — but denied they had asked for the return of the betting slips.

Knightmare Result

After that experience you'd expect me to think twice when approached by a man wishing to bet that, at the age of 38, he would play in a First Division soccer match the next season.

He was quite open about everything - he told me his name, and that he'd played a few games at junior level for a pro club before having to give up the game through injury.

Now, though, his wife was about to publish a book on the powers of self belief combined with a revolutionary new diet.

To support her, he wanted to make a bet to win himself at least £50,000 that he could get into good enough shape to play in the First Division.

He sat in my office for over an hour discussing the bet. I kept suggesting that perhaps we should make the bet seem more realistic by offering odds for him to play in the Vauxhall Conference, then Divisions Four, Three and Two all the way up to Division One.

"No," he insisted, "I'm only interested in Division One."

He went off, asking me to contact him with details of the odds I would be prepared to offer. I liaised with the football compilers in my company and we were all agreed it was virtually impossible for him to do it, but that if he insisted, odds of 10,000-1 might be appropriate - after all, we joked, he might be Kenny Dalglish's brother-in-law for all we knew.

Well, he wasn't, not quite - in fact, he phoned up shortly after just to confirm we were still willing to accept his bet and to say: "I should be able to tell you how much I want to stake in a day or two."

The next day I picked up *The Sun* and read the amazing story of how tycoon Michael Knighton had just bought Manchester United.

The would-be punter who wanted to win £50,000 by playing in the First Division was none other than Mr Knighton! And I believe to this day that if he'd managed to get his bet on, he would have insisted Alex Ferguson pick him for a League game - remember the way he ran out on the pitch juggling the ball in front of the Old Trafford faithful immediately after he'd taken over?

Coming after the Knighton try-on, I had a real feeling of deja-vu when I received a letter from Liverpool florist Ray Thomas asking for a bet that he could play First Division football in season 1991-1992. After making a few enquiries and receiving his solemn word that he was not the son or brother of any current soccer club manager or Chairman, I decided that even if it was some elaborate scam it was worth the risk.

Ray explained that he was in his early thirties and played soccer for a side in a local Liverpool Saturday afternoon league. He had played a few games for Plymouth Reserves some years back and was sick and tired of the lads he played with in the Liverpool League telling him he could have made it if he'd really tried.

Now he wanted to give himself one last opportunity to hit the big time and the bet would be the added incentive he needed. So I laid him a £50 wager at odds of 1000-1 with which he was delighted.

The last I heard of him before this book went to press was that a local TV company had picked up on Ray and were trying to arrange trials for him with Everton!

NS141255

HILL HOUSE, LONDON, SE1 8EJ

Dear Sir,—We confirm having laid you the following at....10.30AM.......on....9th NOVEMBER....19.90

£	P	TO	£	P	ENTRY	Price	Win or 1-2-3	EVENT
50,000	00		50	00	RAY THOMAS	1000/1	WIN	BARCLAYS LEAGUE DIV 1
					TO PLAY IN A BARCLAYS			PARTICIPATION
					LEAGUE DIVISION I MATCH			
					DURING 1991/92 SEASON			
					THE WAGER IS LAID SUBJECT TO THE FOLLOWING CONDITIONS APPLYING AT			
					THE TIME THE BET WAS STRUCK:-			
					a) THAT THE AGE OF MR THOMAS WAS AS STATED (33)			
					b) THAT MR THOMAS WAS NOT SIGNED IN ANY CAPACITY TO A			
					BRITISH FOOTBALL LEAGUE CLUB.			
					TAX PAID			

ALL RETURNS INCLUDING STAKES SUBJECT TO A 10 % DEDUCTION FOR TAX AND LEVY PURPOSES

To........Mr. RAY THOMAS......

A/c No...............................

Checked by

Amount Invested £......55.......:

Yours faithfully,

p.p. William Hill credit Ltd

R.S.

Chapter IV

Taking His Work Home

Thomas Goudie, a £3 per week clerk at the Bank of Liverpool, defrauded his employers of £160,000 - most of which he gambled away to an unscrupulous pair of bookmakers.

The case came to court in February 1902, after Goudie's system of forging cheques was finally rumbled.

Goudie was undetected whilst just betting with bookies Kelly and Stiles, but when three more, Burge, Mances and Marks, also became involved, he stepped up his stakes and at one stage drew £91,000 out of the bank in just three weeks to settle up with the bookies who, not content with winning the money, were now also blackmailing Goudie.

When the business was brought into the open, Mances and Marks contrived to disappear but the other four all stood trial and received heavy penal sentences - Goudie actually died whilst in jail.

Casino Limits

Although British casinos are not allowed to serve alcoholic drinks on the casino floor, the rules are a little different in America's Atlantic City - and a gambler took advantage of that situation to pull something of a stroke on the casino to which he lost £200,000.

In June 1989, Schmuel Aboud successfully counter sued the Golden Nugget casino which was demanding settlement of £20,000 credit he had refused to repay on the grounds that he had been plied with free brandy whilst playing and that this, mixed with drugs he requested from casino staff to kill back pain, made him incapable of proper gambling decisions.

Amazingly, a New Jersey state court ruled that casinos have a responsibility to ensure their customers are sober enough to bet.

Mr Aboud counter sued for the $200,000 he lost at the casino and won the case - leading casino bosses to contemplate introducing breath tests for punters!

Freak Pay Out

A shock result in a three horse race was exploited to the full by forecast backers who had spotted that a massive dividend could accrue if the favourite was out of the frame.

Former Cheltenham Gold Cup winner Little Owl was 4-11 favourite in the Fulwell Chase at Kempton in January 1982. His two opponents were 5-2 shot Venture To Cognac and unconsidered no-hoper Great Dean, 66-1.

Before the race a huge number of forecast bets coupling Venture To Cognac with Great Dean to finish first and second had been placed with all the large bookmakers.

During the race, Little Owl pulled up, leaving Venture To Cognac to come home ahead of Great Dean, with the forecast paying £14.27 for 10p - odds of over 140-1.

After the race the stewards interviewed Little Owl's part-owner and jockey Jim Wilson, and recorded his explanation that he had been unable to steer the horse properly after the bit had come out of the horse's mouth, so had pulled him up.

The bookmakers, stuck with liabilities estimated at £300,000 were not happy, but a BOLA investigation concluded: "There is no reason to withhold payment of certain forecast bets struck on the race."

Colour Blind?

Heinz Kuhl came up with a great plan to beat the bookies in 1976 - he would station himself at Watford dog track, signal the result of the race to his accomplice, Maria Lawrence, the second the dogs went past the post. She would then rush into the betting shop and place a bet on a race which was, unbeknown to the shop as there was usually a delay in notifying the 'off' time of dog races, already over.

They set up their system; Kuhl flashed the result to Lawrence, she rushed into the shop, placed the bet and settled back to await the official confirmation of the result.

Imagine her surprise when the result came through - different from the one she'd backed. Kuhl had got the number of the winning dog wrong!

Trying again, the bungling pair from Shepherds Bush were nabbed - and eventually appeared in court where they were fined, after admitting conspiring to defraud.

Over And Out

Four members of a gang based in the Watford area were convicted in 1977 after using walkie-talkie radios to swindle bookies out of some £250.

Prosecuting, Michael Wilkinson explained how the fraud, based on races at Watford greyhound track, worked:

"As the race finished, the gang member would shin over the fence and would shout the name of the winner to another man in a nearby phone box. He would phone the result to yet another member in a phone box near a bookmaker's shop in or around London. That man would be using a walkie-talkie radio and he could pass the message to a fourth gang member already inside a betting shop. He would have a walkie-talkie radio hidden under his clothes, with an earpiece hidden by a woolly hat. As soon as he got the winning greyhound he would fill in his betting slip, make his bet and collect his winnings. The whole operation from race-track to betting shop could be completed within a minute of the race finishing."

Police filmed the operation taking place to trap those involved in the plot, which relied on late notification of 'off' times or lax staff who assumed that those placing the bet could not possibly be aware of the result.

It must have been difficult to find an empty phone box in Watford in those days!

The Long And The Short Of It

One of the Great Train robbers, Robert Welch, was believed to be the 'brains' behind the Rochester greyhound coup which took place in May 1978.

'The Long and Short Stakes' was an odd contest, which involved two heats run over 277 metres and a final run over 901 metres.

The winners of the two sprint races were 4-1 chance Leysdown Fun and 33-1 shot Leysdown Pleasure. Both had been bought from Ireland and had had their names changed.

The two dogs were heavily backed in a vast number of multiple bets coupling them with every dog in a race at another track, so that all the bets naming them with the winner of that other race were win doubles.

Welch claimed the dogs had been backed in over 200 betting shops and that his winnings added up to £109,000. Other estimates put the total as high as £300,000.

Many bookmakers refused to pay out once details of the coup began to emerge. There were allegations that the starting prices of the two Leysdowns had been artificially manipulated at the track.

Frustrated punters made strenuous efforts to receive payment - the locks of hundreds of betting shops were jammed with super-glue, although those involved with the coup always denied any involvement with this particular campaign.

Police spent years investigating the circumstances of the coup, eventually compiling a two hundred page report.

Only a few bookmakers ever paid out on the coup, with Welch claiming to have received £20,000.

He Who Laughs Last

An Irishman came up with what he considered was the infallible formula for pulling off a major coup on the Eire national lottery.

He even published his method in the form of a book, called *Win The Lotto.*

The book was savaged and rubbished by reviewers.

So Stefan recruited nine friends to form a syndicate to run the system themselves and in April 1990 they won £2,350,000.

Explained syndicate leader and author of the book Stefan Klincewicz: "I knew the system could be managed. It is a simple formula based on mathematics, the law of probability and logic. We began using it three months ago and I selected this group of winning numbers four weeks ago."

The numbers were 17, 28, 29, 32, 36.

Bad Loser

In 1990, when Argentinian punter Victor Rosales was given a hot tip he decided the time had come to pull off a major coup.

So he withdrew his life savings, £10,000, and stuck every last penny on the three-year-old Broncaro, a 12-1 chance.

It ran like a 12-1 chance - finishing last.

So Rosales, who was at the Buenos Aires track to see Broncaro run in the race, walked down to watch the horse come in from the track, pulled out a revolver and shot the horse dead!

A Wing And A Prayer

After doping his fancied big race contender, Londoner John Chipperfield was arrested, charged, and fined £100 in August 1990.

He had given the contender amphetamine sulphate, "because there's a lot of money to be won."

No, he wasn't talking about horse racing - but pigeon racing!

But Racing Pigeon expert Colin Osman thinks he was wasting his time: "Years ago people would give birds tiny doses of arsenic, but the practice of doping has never really caught on. This is because birds are put in baskets on the Friday night before a Saturday race and may not be released until up to 24 hours later, during which time the drug effect would probably have worn off."

Crossed Lines

Nigel Wise, 23, was jailed for two years and Paul Miell, 22, for nine months in June 1975, after admitting conspiring to defraud Ladbrokes.

They planned to intercept and delay the Exchange Telegraph commentary on a greyhound race. Whilst Wise operated the equipment, Miell would go into the betting shop and place a bet.

Miell stole the key to a shop next door to Ladbrokes in Reading, and Wise climbed a telegraph pole to redirect wires from the betting shop into the empty premises. But when they arrived to carry out the coup, the police were waiting for them.

Royal Scandal

In 1791, the Prince of Wales (later King George IV) became caught up in a 'non-trier' scandal.

His retained jockey, Sam Chifney, rode the Prince's Escape, a hot favourite at 1-2, in a race at Newmarket.

Escape finished last of four.

Running the very next day, Escape's previous disappointing display meant that he started at 5-1. Ridden again by Chifney, Escape turned the form upside down by winning the race, beating in the process a horse called Skylark, which had finished well in front of him the day before.

Rumours abounded that the horse hadn't been 'off' on the first occasion so that Chifney could secure better odds for the next race when he had plunged heavily in the betting market. It was even suggested the Prince was in on the ploy. The Stewards called Chifney in to explain himself. Chifney explained that Escape had needed the first race to bring him on for the second. He hadn't backed him at all in the first race, knowing this, and had placed a modest 20 guineas on him the second time.

The Stewards chose not to accept Chifney's explanation and one of them, Sir Charles Bunbury, took it on himself to inform the Prince that, "if Chifney were suffered to ride the Prince's horses, no gentleman would start against him."

The Prince remained loyal to Chifney and announced that he would give up racing, but if he returned to the sport Chifney would train and ride his horses for him.

Added Bonus

In the summer of 1990, a punter from Wakefield, West Yorkshire, went to collect a winning bet for a mate - and ended up being convicted of theft!

The trouble was he should have collected £123.75 from the Coral shop - but the cashier paid him £1237.50 by mistake.

The punter took the money and legged it from the shop, planning to pay his mate what he was due and to keep the rest - but the police nabbed him.

Turf Accounting

Nicholas Young was obsessed with the search for a perfect gambling system - and he spent nearly £11 million looking for it!

Unfortunately for him, most of the £11 million wasn't his to gamble, and in May 1991 he was jailed for four years after admitting eleven deception charges.

The 45-year-old former public schoolboy and Cambridge graduate was earning £34,500 per annum with a City accountancy firm but he persuaded people to invest large amounts of money with him.

When the investors quizzed him about where their money was, Young made an anagram of the word horse and added three more letters, giving his answer in one word - "offshore."

The court heard that in the five years before his arrest Young staked bets totalling £10,922,000 on horses. He won back £8,729,000 in his search for what he described as the "holy grail" of a winning system - leaving him a loss of over £2 million.

Even after he had been arrested Young was still trying to attract more cash for his scheme - he wrote to one investor from his cell offering a copy of his latest betting system, which needed "a copy of the Daily Mirror, a copy of the Times and the odd million in cash".

I wonder if Mr Young is related to my friend Mr Winner, by any chance!

Mug Punters

During an investigation into alleged race-fixing in America between 1969-1971, one of the dubious characters involved, a certain Bobby Byrne, made this memorable comment:

"Most people who bet on horses are suckers. The only winners on the punt are the wise guys - those who either know about the rigged races, or have access to other expert information, drunks who don't know what they're betting on and may get lucky, and little old ladies who use a system of phone numbers or house numbers to select winners."

Trainer's Belief

The inexplicable poor running of hotly fancied Cheltenham Gold Cup contender Playschool, in 1988, has left trainer David Barons convinced that the horse was 'got at'.

In May 1991, he was quoted by *Pacemaker Update* magazine as saying: "I am still convinced Playschool was got at in the Gold Cup; horses should be protected until they get to the paddock. We have never doubted our judgment that Playschool was doped."

Repeat Performance

In 1947 two young students, Albert Hibbs and Roy Walford, caused a sensation when they found a fault in one of the roulette wheels at Reno's Palace Club and, starting with a bank of just $100, won $5000 before the club got wise.

Hibbs, later to become a space scientist and Walford, later a professor of medicine, attracted media attention following their big win - which they then went on to repeat at Harolds Club, where they landed a further $7000 and more publicity.

On The Nose

An ingenious stroke was pulled by an owner which proved literally to be a 'bloody' good coup.

Recalled racing writer Jack Fairfax-Blakeborough in his memoirs: "In 1908, I remember a Malton owner running a horse at Thirsk in a race which looked a gift for him. He was made favourite, but the owner backed the ultimate winner. He had a jockey who was 'paid and did as he was told'. His instructions were to get well away, make the running, and then pull up and dismount a couple of furlongs from home.

At the spot indicated the horse pulled up, the jockey dismounted and the owner, who was standing conveniently near, rushed onto the course. Covered by the jockey he produced from a warm inside pocket a bottle, and with his handkerchief smeared the horse's nostrils with the blood he had that morning collected from a Malton slaughterhouse.

Together, jockey and owner led the horse back to the paddock with blood trickling from its nostrils and the gory handkerchief much displayed. It was obvious for everyone to think that this was a bad case of a blood-vessel breaking.

The following week the same horse ran at another Yorkshire meeting, but no-one except the owner dare take the long odds offered. He won and there was no summons to the stewards room afterwards."

A Long Sentence

I couldn't resist this story of a betting barber which I came across whilst researching. It was in a turn of the century book about gamblers, called *Light Come, Light Go* - by Ralph Nevill.

Apocryphal this tale may be - but it is hugely entertaining, and I prefer to believe it to be true.

"About 1780 there resided at Canterbury a barber who was famous for the way in which he made natty one-curled hunting wigs, but who was also much given to making bets and to boasting of his discernment and judgement.

Two blacklegs, coming to Canterbury for the races, heard of this barber and immediately formed a plan to shave him in his own way. To accomplish the business they went to one of the principal inns, where, ordering a capital supper, they sent for the perruquier to bespeak wigs for themselves and their servants.

The knight of the strop readily and cheerfully attended; and, having taken the external dimensions of the gentlemen's heads, whilst totally ignorant of the schemes which lay within them, was about to depart, but was prevented by a pressing invitation from his new companions to take supper with them.

He was of a convivial turn and fond of company, which in his own opinion afforded opportunities of displaying his great sagacity in the mysteries of betting; and for this reason he politely accepted the invitation.

After supper, a game of whist was suggested, but as the barber did not feel himself so great an adept at this as at his favourite game of 'done and done' the proposal fell to the ground.

As the guest of the evening was a great politician, and his companions were well informed of his manners and character, the conversation turned upon politics - from that, unaccountably veering round till wagers became the general topic.

Highly delighted at the introduction of a subject of which he deemed himself a perfect master, the barber listened with the greatest attention to the conversation and eagerly offered several bets himself.

As his two companions appeared rather shy, and hinted that it would not be safe to bet with a man who calculated matters so shrewdly as generally to win, he became very anxious to get the better of men whom he considered as 'pigeons' - though, unluckily for him they turned out to be 'rooks'.

After many propositions, they offered to bet him ten guineas that he would not repeat one sentence, and that only, during the space of ten minutes.

Cunningly thinking that he had his men, the barber started up and swore he could repeat any sentence for an hour. After having blithely stepped home for a supply of cash, he returned, and a bet of fifty guineas having been made, both stakes were deposited under a hat on the table, the conditions being that the barber should, without interruption, repeat the words 'There he goes' for half an hour's continuance.

He accordingly took his station at the table and, with a watch before him, began his recital of 'There he goes, There he goes....'

When he had kept on in a steady and unalterable tone for a quarter of an hour, one of the gentlemen, with a view to lead the barber from his stated subject, lifted up the hat, counted out half the money, and saying 'D--n me if I don't go' put the cash in his pocket and walked off. This circumstance, however, had no effect upon the barber.

A few minutes later the man who remained, coolly pocketed the residue of the money, and added, as the barber repeated the words, 'There he goes', 'And d--n me if I don't follow him.'

The barber was now left alone with his eyes riveted on the watch, anxious for the expiration of the short time which still remained to elapse before his bet was won, but more confident than ever.

In the meantime, the departure of the two strangers, without settling the bill, excited the notice of the landlord; he went into the room, and the barber, looking him in the face, kept repeating 'There he goes'.

'Yes sir, I know it; they have both been gone some time; pray are you going to pay the bill?'

No answer being given but 'There he goes' the host immediately ran for the barber's wife and a doctor, supposing him in a state of hopeless delerium.

They arrived; his wife, taking him round the neck, in vain endeavoured to make deviate from his purpose; the doctor, after feeling his pulse, pronounced him in a high fever, and was getting ready his apparatus for opening a vein, when the time expired, and the barber, in a frenzy of excitement, jumped upon the table and exclaimed, 'Bravo, I have won fifty guineas of the two gentlemen who are gone out!'

The persons present now concluded, beyond a doubt, that he had lost his senses - his wife screamed, and the landlord called for assistance to have him secured.

When matters were explained however, the landlord had a horse saddled and rode in pursuit of the gentlemen, to remind them of their forgetfulness. After riding about ten miles, he overtook them in a lonely part of the road. Here he reminded them that they had not paid their bill, upon which they presented pistols to his head, robbed him of between 20 and 30 guineas and advised him not to travel again upon such a foolish errand, but to look better after his inn, and tell the barber to be careful how he made his bets in future."

And Not A Cent On!

The FBI came up with a plan which would enable it to crack the race fixing scam which it thought was going on at Finger Lakes, New York in 1989.

They decided to buy themselves a horse which would run badly enough for connections to be approached by the riggers.

The plan went wrong; the horse, Zachregard, cost a mere couple of thousand dollars but promptly ruined the plan - by winning!

Through The Looking Glass

David Gray allegedly single-handedly forced a 'Spot the Ball' competition out of business when he devised an infallible way of backing the winning result.

The 30-year-old Glasgow man won £173,000 when he discovered that by using a magnifying glass he could detect which parts of the pictures used for the game had been doctored by computer in order to remove the ball.

To make sure he covered all the options Gray had to stake £900 - but it was well worth it, as he hit the jackpot in October 1990.

The next week the organisers of the Skilball competition had taken it off the market!

They denied it was because of David's success, saying: "It has been a success but market research showed that many people found the entry procedure too complicated."

But David Gray, who runs a catering business, revealed he had tested his method out previously, and had won £3500. "I knew then it was infallible. It took hours of work and a £900 stake but I knew I was on a certainty."

Ungentlemanly Conduct

Sydney owner-trainer James Kingsley was banned for life after almost getting away with one of the most audacious coups ever perpetrated.

He managed to devise a scam which allowed him to run a horse due to carry 10st 9lbs in a race with just 8st 8lbs on its back - 29lbs difference - turning it from a 20-1 no-hoper to a live contender.

The race took place in April 1903 at Newcastle, Australia. Just before the 'off' Kingsley pounced to literally back his 20-1 shot off the boards. He stood to make £20,000 - about £400,000 by today's values.

The horse, Gentleman Jim, strolled home in the six furlong race and Kingsley rushed back to the weighing out point where there seemed to be a problem with the scales - Gentleman Jim's jockey hadn't made the weight, said a puzzled official.

"Nonsense!" stormed Kingsley, and stamping his foot demanded: "He weighed out right he must weigh in right, put him on again."

Sure enough, the jockey weighed the right amount and the Correct Weight flag was displayed.

Kingsley rushed off to begin collecting his winnings. But the bemused Clerk of the Scales was suspicious, began to check the scales, and discovered a wire running through a hole in the floor.

Lifting up the floorboards the Clerk and the Stewards discovered the wire ran down to a 29lb lump of lead and a young boy concealed in a small hole where he had been placed the night before with instructions that when he heard Kingsley stamp his foot he should attach the weight to the wire!

The game was up.

Cottoning On

One of the most notorious 'ringer' cases in Australian racing history took place in August 1984, when a horse called Fine Cotton won at Brisbane's Eagle Farm Track, landing a massive gamble.

The horse had been quoted at an opening price of 33-1 which tumbled to 7-2. Sydney bookies held liabilities of over half a million dollars; Brisbane bookies were in for just under 200,000 dollars; Sydney credit bookmaker Mark Read was facing a $163,000 payout.

Fortunately for them, sadly for the perpetrators of the coup, it transpired that Fine Cotton was in fact a more than useful horse called Bold Personality.

Owner John Gillespie and trainer Hayden Haitana were convicted of being behind the attempted sting which netted Gillespie a four year jail sentence and Haitana a twelve month one.

If At First You Succeed...

Perhaps one of the most persistent of people involved in ringer cases in Australia is Melbourne jockey Stephen Wood who, in 1972, rode a top sprinter called Regal Vista (running as Royal School) to land a betting coup and then ten years later found himself involved in THREE ringer cases within fourteen months.

He ended up in jail.

Gold Fill In

A quick thinking pools punter won himself £50,000 and made the pools companies change their rules, when he spotted a loophole in the system in February 1970.

London dentist Sydney Lewis realised that with thirty games postponed because of the weather, and the 'Pools Panel' of experts who predict the results of games not called into action - at the time they only operated when there were 31 games off - he was in a great position to make a full cover entry for the remaining matches and be able to guarantee himself first dividend payouts.

By notifying a pools agent in time to place his bet - having previously supplied him with a blank cheque - just a couple of hours before kick off time he was able to outwit the rules - and be confident that hundreds of thousands of entries would already be in from punters who were unaware of how many games would be called off when they placed their bets.

With just 24 matches remaining on the Vernons Coupon he had chosen for his coup, Mr Lewis required an outlay of £1600 to cover every possible combination of eight results - and duly cleaned up with nine first dividends and a host of smaller ones to win £50,000.

But in a way Mr Lewis had done the pools companies a favour - the six major firms immediately got together to make sure nothing similar could ever happen again.

Chapter V

Divine Intervention?

In 1990, I decided that William Hill should open a book on the identity of the new Archbishop of Canterbury, following the news that the current incumbent was to retire.

The book went well with a lively turnover of bets.

Suddenly, in late July, there was a rush of bets for the then 20-1 shot George Carey, Bishop of Bath, whose odds shortened dramatically to as low as 2-1 before the betting book was closed - followed almost immediately by the announcement that George Carey had, indeed, got the job.

The next day the tabloid newspapers were full of stories about betting bishops and clandestine clergy having made a few ungodly gains by cashing in on inside knowledge about the identity of the new Archbishop by placing bets with their local bookies.

The Reverend Carey himself was reported as saying: "Somebody leaked the news, but it certainly wasn't one of us (meaning his family). Some people have said a lot of church roofs are going to be repaired, but they won't be in Bath and Wells."

I am pleased to be able to reassure the Archbishop. In fact it was not the clergy who pulled off the coup; it was, though, newspaper reporters themselves who did - they and their pals.

And how did they do it?

Well, my enquiries have revealed that the papers were supplied with an embargoed release about George Carey's appointment some hours before the news was made public - but in plenty of time to pop down to the bookies and to then be able to think up a way of covering their tracks by blaming punting parsons!

Fortunately for my firm one of my very best national newspaper contacts was honest enough to let me know what was going on - we were able to close our books before significant damage was done - unlike our less clued-in competitors!

State Benefits

Conning the bookies is difficult enough, but conning a bookie and the Department of Health and Social Security probably deserves a medal!

I had to look twice at the letter I received from a punter who said he was a patient in a Liverpool hospital and that he wanted to make a

Grand National bet.

The letter had arrived a couple of weeks prior to the big race, and with it had come a cheque for £220 which was, explained the would-be punter, the stake money for his bet. He would ring me on the day of the race and tell me which horse he wished to back.

Fair enough, you might think, but the extraordinary thing was the cheque was made out to William Hill Ltd - and issued by the DHSS!

Just how the patient had managed to persuade them to make out a cheque to a bookmaker, for a bet he hadn't even placed, really beggars belief - but when I contacted the particular DHSS office involved, they insisted to me that this was impossible - until I sent them a photo-copy of the cheque.

And no, I didn't place the bet, but wrote to the punter informing him we would need a personal cheque to be able to accede to his wishes.

An Inside Job

There must be something about the Grand National, because in 1991 I came across a communication which had all the hallmarks of being an audacious attempt at a con.

The letter, and a covering note, had originally been sent to one of the two daily trade papers and it outlined a scheme which the writer claimed was to be attempted at one of our Northern betting shops on Grand National day - I don't intend to explain the precise details of the scheme for fear of encouraging someone else to have a crack at it, but suffice to say in theory it had some plausibility, although I am very doubtful that it would have been workable in practice.

Anyway, the scheme revolved around a little bit of inside assistance and it appeared to be this angle which had upset my correspondent:

"To be frank, I do not really care about Hills but I do wish to prevent one person being involved just in case something does go wrong."

Having excited our interest with the details of the attempted coup and then made us feel he was obviously a decent type of bloke who was concerned about the welfare of a mate, the anonymous writer then got down to what to me seemed to be the crux of the matter:

"If you have negotiated a reward with Hills for the enormous help I have given them then I will contact you later to arrange for an innocent courier to collect it from you."

Yes, I bet he would!

We turned down this possible blackmail attempt.

Irish Joke

Rock star Sting once told me how he had been conned into buying a racehorse by half a dozen Irish builders who had been working on his house. "Sting," they said, "what you need with all your money is a whole string of racehorses."

And they just happened to have one for him - it was called Sweetcal. With no knowledge of the sport, Sting was surprised to eventually discover that his new purchase was not very highly rated - but he had the last laugh when Sweetcal won races at 33-1 and 14-1.

Cheep Tricks

When I was approached about offering odds for the likelihood of someone being able to breed a pink budgerigar, little did I believe that there could be any untoward angle on such a proposition.

However, I soon had a rude awakening - apparently a pink budgerigar would ensure virtual immortality for the man or woman who could breed it. No-one has ever yet managed it.

But little did I realise what would happen when breeders became aware of the 100-1 odds being offered by William Hill against it happening - I took scores of bets and within a few weeks claims began flooding in.

I had stipulated that any claims must ultimately be verified by the British Budgerigar Society and I was staggered when their Arthur Bracey filled me in on the lengths punters had been prepared go to 'win' their 100-1 wagers. "We've had people bring us birds covered in brick dust, birds who've been dyed and birds who've been rubbed against iodine blocks," revealed Mr Bracey.

He also related how one audacious attempt to con the adjudicators by means of food colouring was only exposed after they kept the bird long enough for it to moult, revealing its true colours.

Not So Silly-Billys

From budgies to babies - I only hope these stories don't get me into trouble with people in high places - but I'm convinced we were conned when I persuaded the company to let me open a book on the name of Prince Charles's and Princess Di's first-born.

We priced up all the traditional Royal names like Charles, James, Edward, George etc but for some reason offered 20-1 about William. Sure enough, along came a certain day when all of a sudden, within the space of about half an hour, several of our branches in the Westminster area were visited by previously unknown punters, all plunging a few quid on the likelihood that the potential future King would be called Billy.

The odds nose-dived until William was favourite - we were about to suspend the book when the official news was announced: "Royal baby to be called William."

Double Trouble

It looked very much like something similar was happening in April 1984 when, with Princess Di pregnant again, there was a flurry of bets up to £750 at 50-1 that she would be having twins.

The news that we had closed the book made the front pages of several tabloid papers on 3 April, but to my relief, and despite the fact that one of my best newspaper contacts had told me identical cots had been delivered to the Palace, it transpired she was only having a single baby - but who knows what chance remarks overheard or passed on can lead to inside information leaving the bookies vulnerable.

The *Daily Express* for 3 April certainly thought something was up and in a front page story told readers: "Speculation that Princess Diana is expecting twins grew late last night after a £250,000 betting coup was stopped by a top bookmaker. William Hill dramatically shut their book on the baby's sex yesterday after six anonymous punters tried to put large amounts on twin births."

I was relieved at the outcome of that particular confinement and even more so when I was told a day in advance of the official announcement that the first-born of the Duke and Duchess of York was to be named Beatrice. I had that name at 100-1 in my list and if the person who told me had decided to keep quiet and just had a bet it could have resulted in a Bea-sting for the bookies!

Another potential Royal sting could have been in its early throes even as this book was being prepared. I have been approached by several punters, and laid a number of bets at odds of 100-1, down to 50-1 that Prince Charles will renounce his right to the throne before the end of 1992.

You read it here first!

Told You!

Whether the client who wrote to me from Clevedon, Avon in October 1990 was trying to con me I suppose I will never know, but his letter asked for odds that, "Namibia will be a member of the Commonwealth by 31st March 1992".

It was already a member!

Hit Man

Not quite as blatant as that piece of inside information was the £10 bet which a Mr Parsons of London placed with me at odds of 50-1 in January 1991, when he asked for odds about punk group The Clash having a number one hit single within a year.

Mug that I am, I decided a bunch of has-been punks had no chance of making the charts again, so I was mildly surprised to learn the record chosen to launch a multi-million pound advertising campaign to promote Levi's jeans was called Should I Stay Or Should I Go - by The Clash.

It soared to number one within three weeks of release.

I paid Mr Parsons ruefully and he was honest enough to admit to me that he had had "an inkling" that The Clash record might be chosen for this particular campaign - oh well, at least no-one else backed it.

It has always been a dicey business betting on the charts but I like to run a book on what will be the Christmas Number One - even though I now find that cunning record pluggers have taken to trying to stake large amounts on 'no-hope' records just to get them into my list of short-odds shots and thereby encourage publicity for them.

I got wise to that one a couple of years back when the men behind an absolutely dreadful dirge of a record by a well known actor had plunged hundreds of quid on the record at odds of 500-1, backed it again when we went 100-1 and kept on backing it until we had it as 5-2 favourite.

It sold about a dozen copies and reached number 578 in the charts - but they were delighted with the publicity they received.

Nowadays I reckon to be able to spot the 'non-triers' so we just take the money and knock the price out!

At Christmas 1989, we were definitely targeted when insiders somehow discovered that the Band Aid track Do They Know It's Christmas? was guaranteed to be the Xmas Chart topper and started trying to place bets of up to £10,000!

It was fortunate that they were so greedy. Had they confined themselves to small bets they may have been able to get on - but when strangers turn up looking for four and five figure bets on an event which normally attracts £50 flutters, then the alarm bells pretty soon ring.

We were able to close the book without coming to too much harm - but fancy trying to con us over a charity record; I'm sure the conmen behind the scam wouldn't have been donating their winnings to the Band Aid appeal.

Monster Bets

Changing the subject slightly, I've had a lot of fun with bets on the likelihood or otherwise of the Loch Ness Monster being proved conclusively to exist.

The current odds at time of going to press are 500-1 against, with any proof which is produced having to be verified by the Natural History Museum's Iain Bishop.

In October 1990, I organised the William Hill Monster Hunt Weekend - offering a reward of £250,000 for anyone who could come up with conclusive proof of the existence of Nessie during a three day, Friday to Sunday period.

Despite the best efforts of Screaming Lord Sutch to entice the Beastie out with haggis-smeared British Rail sandwiches, a bid utilising the psychic powers of crystals, plus some of the most advanced high technology sonar scanning equipment available, no-one came up with the necessary proof - or so I thought until I received a letter from a Mr B.P.Berlanny of Portsmouth.

"I am writing to officially claim the £250,000 offered by William Hill for sighting the Loch Ness Monster," wrote Mr Berlanny, going on to reveal he had spotted and photographed Nessie, "...in early August at about 4pm on the West Bank of Loch Lomond, looking in a northerly direction towards Loch Ness."

And he enclosed a copy of a photograph he'd taken, which showed Nessie FLYING above the Loch! (Sadly, in the opinion of the printers it is not good enough to reprint here.)

"The explanation for this phenomenon is quite simple. Nessie is a very intelligent creature and she has certain special characteristics of disguise."

Mr Berlanny closed his letter by commenting: "I look forward to being advised that I have won your offered prize."

Well, of course I showed Mr Berlanny's photograph to my expert, Iain Bishop, who diplomatically proferred his opinion that it wasn't exactly sufficiently convincing enough for him to advise me to pay out the quarter of a million - which was a relief!

However, if any of you out there think you have a good reason to believe that Nessie does exist then let me know - because William Hill still have a £20,000 prize available for conclusive proof.

By the way, Project Urquhart, supported by TV news reader Nicholas Wichell, hopes to unravel some of Loch Ness's mysteries in a four-year period from 1992-96.

∞ ∞ ∞

Iain Bishop saved me from a payout on a similar occasion, too - when mountaineer Chris Bonington backed himself at 150-1 to return from a climbing expedition to Mount Menlungtse in the Himalayas with conclusive proof of the existence of the Yeti, or Abominable Snowman.

Well, Chris is one of nature's gentlemen, and far from being any kind of conman, but on his return he brought back what he considered to be useful evidence in favour of the case for the Yeti.

I put Chris and Iain together and the latter examined the evidence, which included what Chris claimed might well be the first ever samples of Yeti droppings to be discovered.

Iain was eager to take them for further investigation but, sadly for everyone and for Chris's chances of winning his tenner bet, the droppings were confiscated by a couple of large men from the Ministry of Agriculture and Fish who suddenly arrived on the scene demanding to know how the droppings had been smuggled into the country!

They took them away and, I believe, promptly burnt them - thus disposing of a rare opportunity to check out some apparently first hand evidence.

Chapter VI

Clock-Watching

Slot machines, or one-armed bandits, account for an astronomical turnover of gambling cash each year - but in 1949, the industry, already booming, faced the threat of bankruptcy thanks to a system of playing the machines developed by a player in Las Vegas who had appeared from nowhere.

Quite brazenly, in front of casino owners and inspectors, the player began to empty slot machines of their jackpots.

Within a week he had won over 300 jackpots and collected some $30,000.

The player began to pass on his system, known as the Rhythm Method, to other players.

Jake Kozloff, then owner of the Las Vegas Golden Nugget casino, learned the method and wagered $10,000 with a slot manufacturer's representative that he could empty any machine he cared to put in front of him. To the amazement and concern of the man, Kozloff achieved this within 20 minutes.

During 1949, it was estimated that rhythm players and syndicates took half a billion dollars off the casinos.

American gambling expert John Scarne investigated the system. In his book *Complete Guide To Gambling*, he wrote:

"How did the original mysterious stranger happen to come up with his bright idea? And who was he? I did some further detective work and discovered that he was an Idaho farmer who, during his spare time, had been helping a slot-mechanic friend repair out of order machines.

He discovered that the three wheels in certain makes of machine made exactly the same number of revolutions when the handle was pulled. He studied the clock fan, which controls the length of time the reels spun, and found that on some machines the clock went dead from seven to eight seconds after the reels stopped spinning.

He also memorised the position of each symbol on each reel. In actual play, since he knew the relative positions on the reel of all the symbols, he could deduce from the nine visible symbols he could see through the window just where all the others were.

Then, by timing himself to pull the machine's level at precisely the right instant, and before the clock gear went dead, he found he could manipulate the desired symbols onto the pay line."

By 1950, a pamphlet explaining this method was on sale for $5 a throw - the industry was in disarray!

However, all good things must come to an end - particularly if they mean that the casino operators have lost out on their 'edge' over the players.

The slot machine industry set its finest brains to work twenty four hours a day and, by 1951, a new gimmick had been added to the mechanism of the machines - a variator, a mechanical device which controlled the clock mechanism so that the spin started at different times.

The bandit bonanza was over.

Taken For A Ride

'The Hiker', a con-man and card player of the twenties, used to fleece fellow diners in Lindy's Restaurant in New York with an ingenious scam.

At the end of a meal he would offer to 'toss' his companion for the cost of the meal plus an additional fifty dollars.

The Hiker would toss a nickel and say: "Call while it's in the air."

His companion would call "Tails". And down it would come - Heads.

The Hiker never lost at this scam - he didn't always win, but he certainly never lost.

How come?

He had a double-headed coin. If the fellow diner called Tails then he couldn't win.

If he called Heads then The Hiker would catch the coin before it fell and drop it in his pocket, laughing and saying, "No bet, I was just testing out your sporting blood, we'll go halves in the bill."

The Hiker enjoyed plenty of freebie meals!

Bloody Good Idea

A Newmarket trainer was determined not to have to sell his promising horse once it had landed a gamble in a selling race at Warwick - so he gave his stable lad a syringe filled with pig's blood, and after the horse had duly obliged, the lad swiftly squirted blood all over the horse's nose and on the jockey's silks.

Of course all potential buyers thought the horse had burst a blood vessel and declined to bid for it.

The Ideal Weighting Race

Jump jockey Barry Brogan claimed to have landed a £17,000 gamble by riding a horse to victory at Carlisle carrying ten pounds less than the allotted weight.

Apparently, according to author Brian Radford in his book *Taken For A Ride*, Brogan had weighed out carrying the correct amount of weight but nipped in to the toilet on his way to mount up, removed ten pounds of lead from his lead cloth and then slipped it under an old potato sack, which he had conveniently left lying around.

He had ridden the horse - which he had arranged to bet £10,000 on - to a comfortable victory, before coming back to weigh-in and picking up the extra weight from under the sack before he sat on the scales.

Globe Trotting

Brisbane-based mare Trance found more than her fair share of trouble during her racing career in the late nineteenth century - and may well be able to claim the dubious honour of being the most disqualified horse of all time.

In 1892, Trance was disqualified for life and her owner and trainer also warned off when she was found guilty of being a non- trier in the Brisbane Cup.

Trance was sold and shipped to Victoria, where the new owner managed to have her disqualification withdrawn. She started racing again, only to be involved in controversy when she was accused of being switched with another - inferior - horse, to win two races in one day.

Trance was sold again and ended up in England. She was soon in trouble and disqualified from racing yet again - this time for 'inconsistent running'.

The globe-trotting Trance next appeared in the States where, after being used as a ringer, she was given another life disqualification!

Then, to cap it all, it was reported in the media that Trance had died while giving birth to a foal - but she hadn't. She was actually sold to a German stud where she took up residence for breeding purposes.

Pride Comes Before A Fallon

The greatest ever single betting coup on one race was almost certainly the Druid's Lodge Confederacy's astonishing triumph over Hackler's Pride in the 1903 Cambridgeshire.

They reportedly collected £250,000 - a staggering £10.5 million in today's equivalent - after the horse stormed home by three lengths.

The Confederacy consisted of a group of five specialists who came together with the express purpose of relieving the bookies of substantial amounts of cash, and consistently achieved just that.

The five were: City financier Percy Cunliffe; Irish stud owner and West End impresario Wilfred Purefoy; celebrated huntsman Frank Forester; Edward Wigan, wealthy in his own right from his family's hop merchants business; and Irish vet and stud manager Holmer Peard.

The five installed the brilliant, young Irish trainer Jack Fallon in specially constructed stables on Salisbury Plain _ away from prying eyes. This was Druid's Lodge.

Here the syndicate built up a powerful stable of horses, which they aimed at all manner of races, from sellers to classics.

But the genius of their system was that the outside world rarely knew just which race was a Druid's Lodge horse's true target. They were not above running horses over the wrong distances, short of fitness and with the deliberate intention of being beaten if it suited their purposes. They were also brilliant at spreading their betting money about to confuse the betting market.

They had many coups before and after, but the Hackler's Pride 1903 Cambridgeshire perhaps represented the pinnacle of the Druid's Lodge achievements.

Hackler's Pride was acquired by Druid's Lodge in 1902, under the ownership of Frank Forester, after being 'spotted' in Ireland by Holmer Peard. She impressed everyone and was aimed at a valuable five furlong race at the end of the season, which she won in some style.

1903 plans were fluid as the stable considered the options. She first raced as a three-year-old at Sandown in April; running unfit, she finished out of the places in a 16 runner sprint.

In June they tried her in a mile race and she finished a close up second to a decent winner, conceding four pounds and still well below true fitness.

This was the crucial stage at which the Cambridgeshire was nominated as the horse's main target for the season.

The filly next ran in a competitive sprint, the Wokingham, in which there was no intention that she should make any impression at all, and she didn't.

She was also entered in the Stewards Cup, another sprint, in which she was an early ante-post fancy. Hackler's Pride finished in a moderate midfield placing.

Now an intensive training programme was introduced at home for the horse, which was allotted 7st 1lb when the Cambridgeshire weights were announced.

Connections were delighted. On their calculations it made Hackler's Pride the proverbial 'good thing' at the weights if reproducing her best form - which very few people were aware of, certainly not the handicappers!

Now they had to get their money down. A network of unlikely but trustworthy punters and agents was used by the Confederacy to get on - even a local parish priest in the Birmingham area was involved.

Hackler's Pride was quoted at very long odds when the first ante-post market was formed, and at this stage the whole coup almost fell apart as trainer Fallon helped himself to the odds without informing his partners. Purefoy threatened to withdraw the horse before the row was smoothed over.

In mid October, Hackler's Pride was a 25-1 chance - the stable had been backing other horses in order to cover their tracks as they continued to place the 'real' money.

The first inkling to the general public of what was going on came when the *Sporting Luck* newspaper reported that the horse had been backed to win "something like £10,000" (the equivalent of almost £450,000 today).

Now the gloves were off and the money began to pour on from all possible sources.

But an unexpected hitch suddenly arose - no train could be found to take Hackler's Pride from London, where she had been sent with the stable's other entries for the race, to Newmarket. Calamity!

In the end palms had to be greased to provide a special train to take the horses up to Newmarket.

Hackler's Pride was still being backed on the day of the race, from 8-1 to 6-1, which made her second favourite behind Kilglass at 9-2.

Even at this stage, strokes were being pulled and Jack Jarvis, who had been listed to ride another of the stable's horses, was suddenly told he would be aboard Hackler's Pride.

The filly was so tuned up and eager to go, she almost bolted with her jockey, only for a stable lad, sent down to the start to calm the animal, to run out on the course and call to her - slowing her down and allowing Jarvis to regain control.

The race itself was little more than a formality. "I was one of the first away, and after a hundred yards I never saw another horse in the race," said Jarvis. The pair won by three lengths.

Only after the race did the bookmakers begin to learn just what a coup had been perpetrated.

Cunliffe revealed that his commission agent, Arthur Hamblin, had £63,000 (£2.75 million today) to hand over to him.

Fallon admitted to winnings of £32,000 (over £1.25 million).

Purefoy had backed the horse countrywide. There were huge winnings to come from overseas wagers and private commissions. One of the men used to place bets for the stable, a station master, William Murray, won between £4-5000 himself (up to £200,000 today).

Incredibly, in 1904, Hackler's Pride was once more aimed at the Cambridgeshire - and again won it, being backed from 33-1 to 7-2 joint favourite and winning by a neck.

Once again the winnings were enormous, if not quite as big as 1903. The *Winning Post* newspaper reported: "The Druid's Lodge stable have landed a great coup; one of the biggest this establishment has ever succeeded in winning."

The Druid's Lodge Confederacy continued to make life difficult for the nation's bookmakers (and handicappers) until the First World War brought it to an end.

Twisting Lane

A double-bluff scheme involving the ringer that wasn't caused a riot in New South Wales, Australia in the 1820s.

A Captain Lane owned a champion racer called Hector, which was entered at the Regentville track.

The Captain, who had been strongly suspected of using Hector as a ringer in other races, put it around that the horse he would actually be running would not be Hector, but another horse called Cripple, disguised to look like Hector; and that the good Captain would be backing a horse called Bennelong.

In fact, the Captain was doing no such thing - it was the real Hector in the race.

But, cunningly, the Captain ensured that Hector finished down the field in his first heat, finishing third and just scraping into the run-off (this was how races were conducted in Aussie in those days).

Now, of course, everyone was convinced that Bennelong must be an absolute certainty - that was until, just before the off, there was a sudden rush of support for Hector which saw his odds tumble to joint favouritism. It was the Captain's money of course, and Hector duly stormed to victory.

But the result sparked off an absolute riot between the deluded punters and the Captain and his accomplices. In the end soldiers had to be called in to split up the warring factions and calm matters down, by which time the Captain was long gone - having disappeared off down the road on board Hector!

Landed In Their Lap

In May 1930, Champion Aussie superstar Phar Lap was matched with a moderate opponent, Fruition, in a warm up race in Adelaide.

The race was a formality - some bookies actually offered 1000-1 against Fruition, others 500-1 ON Phar Lap.

However, a group of shrewd punters managed to pull off a considerable coup in one of the first ever tote rigging cases on record.

They place bets at Tote odds on Phar Lap with Starting Price bookies, many of them strictly illegal. Then, just before the race, plunged £100 on Fruition on the course totalisator.

With virtually no money being bet on Phar Lap because of the obviously restrictive odds being anticipated, the Fruition odds came tumbling down, with the result that Phar Lap was actually returned at 1-3 - remarkable odds for a 1-500 shot!

Phar Lap sauntered home by five lengths.

Blind Bend

For bare-faced cheek the scam pulled by a gang on Derby Day in 1933, and related by former racecourse security chief W.Bebbington in his 1939 book *Rogues Go Racing*, takes some beating.

"In 1933 a gang of racing crooks engineered and successfully carried out one of the greatest welshing coups of recent years. They selected Derby Day and very ingeniously constructed a portable totalisator on the chassis of an old lorry (hired locally at a cost of thirty shillings).

After they had completed their job there was no semblance of a motor lorry, for the structure had been lavishly camouflaged with a display of posters, flags and banners.

Separate windows were available for the sale of 5/- (25p), 10/- and £1 tickets, and the 'operators' were there, smartly attired in clean white smocks; some wore horn-rimmed glasses with tinted lenses as an aid to disguise.

The gang had very carefully chosen a site adjacent to the 'St Dunstans' Derby Day Service' party enclosure at Tattenham Corner. The whole business had undoubtedly been thought out and everything worked according to plan.

The St Dunstans' tote, as the swagger notices indicated, was only doing business on the big race, and the staff were certainly kept very busy at the selling windows, right up to the start of the big event.

Situated in such a popular area, it quickly became a great centre of attraction, and the one amusing side to this swindle was that members of the Metropolitan Police, noticing the crowd and congestion, came up and volunteered to control the flow of patrons by the formation of queues!

Eventually the 'off' was signalled and down went the 'tote' windows with a bang. The crowd rushed away to view the race, leaving the 'tote' operators to prepare the dividends.

After the race had been decided, the successful investors then returned, and under police supervision formed queues in anticipation of receiving their winnings.

Unfortunately the 'boys of the village' were no longer there to perform this service. During the race they had very quietly taken their departure and the pool, which, I was informed at some later date, amounted to approximately £1600."

Tap The Wink

A Scottish punter shocked the racing world in March 1991, when he claimed he had made almost a quarter of a million pounds by betting on information he had obtained by tapping into conversations on mobile phones used by trainers, jockeys, bookmakers and punters.

The *Racing Post* told how the anonymous punter had contacted them wanting to sell his bugging equipment, as well as tapes of conversations between racing people discussing horses.

The mystery man, who called himself Philip, told the paper's Tim Richards that he had a small piece of machinery resembling a portable

phone which could be programmed to intercept the airways used by mobile phones.

"My brother and I have been driving into racecourse car parks and listening to the conversations of the racing people and marking off the relevant horses. I would say I have made more than £200,000 over the last nine months."

'Philip' played Richards a tape recording over the phone, "of a person closely connected with a big stable putting £150 on a horse for himself and £150 for the stable jockey." The horse they backed won at 4-9, reported the Post.

'Philip' then offered to meet Richards at Carlisle racecourse and to sell his equipment for, "in the region of £20,000." He told Richards: "Come to Carlisle and we will make some money together. But I don't want to be messed about so you must bring payment in readies. You can have everything and I don't want anything else to do with it."

He claimed to have set up a legitimate business on his profits from the bets he had made and that he was going to settle in America.

Richards said: "The meeting did not take place."

Lillee In The Pink

A contemporary example of a world famous player backing the opposition to win occurred in July 1981 and involved Dennis Lillee in a storm of controversy, although no-one, surely, could doubt the absolute dedication to winning displayed by the fiery fast bowler during his career - especially against England.

But it was England who he and, allegedly, team-mate Rodney Marsh staked £10 on when he learned they were being offered at odds of 500-1 to come back from a seemingly impossible position to beat the Aussies at Headingley.

Lillee was playing in the game, in which England had followed on and were six for one in their second innings.

Lillee staked his bet, England made 356, Lillee taking three wickets. They then bowled the Aussies out for III (Lillee made 17) to win the game!

Lillee won £5000.

Telegram Scam

At the turn of the century bookmakers would accept bets by telegram, providing they were date-stamped before the 'off' time of the race.

A newspaper of the day *The Winning Post* described how a coup was pulled off by trainer Captain Percy Bewicke and stockbroker G.A.Prentice with a two-year-old, Stratton, in a race at Nottingham:

"A little village was found. A small shop was discovered in it, which had added to its everyday affairs that of a telegraph office. At a given moment, a huge bundle of telegrams were handed in, piled on top of one another, to back Stratton, addressed to various bookmakers scattered all over England. Well, how plain it all is! One female telegraphic operator, one instrument, and sheaves of wires! Result? Stratton won at 10-1. The bookmakers were congratulating themselves at not laying the winner, when the wires began to come in - and they continued to pour in till nightfall."

The above scheme was as nothing compared with that operated by the gang of punters who went to the lengths of purchasing a post office of their own, and then setting their own times in its telegraph machine - a licence to print money!

Sweet Victory

American gambler John 'Bet you a million' Gates collected 11,000 dollars from a wealthy friend, John Drake.

They had bet on whose bread, dunked in coffee, would attract the most flies.

Gates had 'forgotten' to mention that he had put six spoonfuls of sugar in his own cup!

Haydn Sick

According to legend, the composer Wolfgang Amadeus Mozart once bet fellow musician Haydn a case of champagne that Haydn could not play at sight a piece he, Mozart, had just composed.

Haydn accepted the wager and began to play, only to stop short upon reaching a section which prescribed playing with the two hands, one at either end of the keyboard, whilst striking a note in the centre.

Haydn admitted defeat and concede the wager, whereupon Mozart took over at the keyboard and played the piece through. When he reached the vital note, he bent forward and played it with his nose.

Plain Sailing

American writer and wit Wilson Mizner hit on a way of conning fellow passengers during a cruise.

A favourite form of entertainment for the wealthy cruisers was a daily lottery in which they had to estimate the number of miles the ship covered during a day.

Mizner thought he had detected signs of fallibility in an officer with access to the ship's log so, cunningly, he positioned himself outside the officer's cabin and discussed, rather loudly with an accomplice, the number he had drawn, concluding: "You know what I'd do if I won? I'd stick a thousand bucks under the right officer's pillow."

Sure enough, when the number was announced, Mizner had won.

He and his accomplice pulled the same stroke again and tried it once more, stationing themselves outside the cabin door, only to hear a voice growl, "Clear off, you bastards, I'm four hundred miles off course already."

Dead Unlucky

If this story isn't true, it certainly should be!

William Crockford, founder of the casino, owned the second favourite for the 1844 Derby, Ratan. However, so the story goes, he expired just a couple of days before the race was to be run.

This presented his friends, who had all plunged heavily on the horse, with a problem - under the rules of the day, if the owner of a horse died then the horse had to be scratched from any races it was entered in.

Crockford's pals came up with the idea of propping his lifeless body up at the window of his club, where passers-by would see it and assume that all was well. This they did - only for the plan to misfire when Ratan could only manage to finish down the field.

Wheel Change

A Yorkshire mechanic, William Jaggers, came up with a system which eventually won him a reported £80,000 profit from the Monte Carlo Casino at the turn of the century.

Jaggers employed half a dozen assistants for a month's duration, in the course of which they did nothing but check the numbers which came up on different wheels at different tables.

At the end of the month Jaggers was able to detect slight but distinct tendencies towards certain numbers on certain wheels. He and his assistants became so familiar with the wheels they were able to follow them from table to table.

Eventually the Casino decided their only chance of beating Jaggers was to have completely new wheels constructed, which they did, managing to regain some of their losses.

But Jaggers was nothing if not a realist and once the tide turned against him he called a halt, satisfied with his remaining £80,000 winnings.

And Here's One We Prepared Earlier

The story is also told of the late nineteenth century con which led to the Monte Carlo Casino doing away with white-backed packs of cards, in favour of patterned ones.

Apparently a meticulously organised sting took place when a card table was suddenly disrupted one evening by an altercation between two players, during the course of which a large amount of money was suddenly, and apparently accidentally, swept on to the floor.

The confusion was eventually smoothed over when all the money was collected up, and the game continued.

But it soon became obvious that a number of big players had suddenly appeared in the frame and large amounts were being staked on certain combinations of cards - all of which were suddenly appearing.

The Casino was being taken to the cleaners by the time the authorities realised and called a halt to play on that table.

It later transpired that the gang involved had arranged the altercation, having bribed a croupier, who, whilst the confusion was at its height, slipped a ready prepared pack of cards which he then brought into play, with inevitable results.

As a result the Casino in future changed the packs of cards used each day and used different designs to avoid such a marked or rigged deck being introduced so easily in the future - not that that prevented many from trying!

Green Opponents

Golf is a game which lends itself to gambling - but a player who has just lost a few quid to another whom he believes to be 'a bandit', or to have under or over-estimated his true handicap, may be interested to know that such dubious practices, designed to turn the odds against the honest player, have been around for ever.

Or, at least, since 1687, when one Thomas Kincaid wrote in The Book Of The Old Edinburgh Club: "I thought upon the question whither it is better in giveing advantage in gameing to make the game aequell and the stakes unaequall, or to make the stakes aequall and give some advantage in the game - to give a man two holes of three, laying aequall stakes, or to lay three stakes to his one and play aequall for so much every hole."

Kincaid concluded that if you were taking on a superior player you should use a handicap method to overcome him, but if you were facing a lesser talent the best ruse was to offer him generous odds to make him think he had a chance of landing a big win.

Eyes Down, Look Out

A Roman Catholic priest was ostensibly organising harmless, church-sponsored bingo evenings, raising a few dollars for his Indiana church.

In actual fact he was running a high-powered, £1.2 million per year illegal bingo operation, which saw him jailed for 10 months in May 1991.

Monsignor John Morales's operation raked in up to £60,000 per night as he bussed in players from three states. Coaches would be parked a mile away from the Steelworkers McBride Hall to avoid attracting attention, and each night armed guards would accompany the organisers in a motorcade as they banked the takings.

Each high stakes game was publicised as a fund-raiser for

Morales's church, and the paid workers were told to say they were volunteers.

Morales was found guilty of operating an illegal gambling business and conspiring to prevent the government from collecting taxes.

He said: "I ask the forgiveness of everyone to whom I have caused pain or shame. I have tried in 31 years of priesthood to teach respect for the laws."

District Judge Allen Sharp commented: "There are bingo games and there are bingo games. And it didn't take much to figure out this was more than a little old bingo game."

Blazing Row

Tens of thousands of partisan supporters had flocked to London's Lillie Bridge stadium, then Britain's premier athletics venue, in September 1887 to see the sprint showdown between Londoner Harry Hutchens and Geordie Harry Gent.

It had been dubbed 'the Race of the Century' and hundreds of thousands of pounds had been staked in bets with the bookmakers who thronged the arena.

But, unbeknown to the spectators, the managers of the two runners had agreed between themselves to fix the result of the race so they could land a major betting coup.

Unfortunately for them, when the two runners learned of this plan they both refused to have anything to do with it - and quit the stadium.

Word began to spread and the crowd became a rampaging mob which began to riot - eventually burning down and totally destroying the stadium.

An Offer He Couldn't Refuse

A Yugoslav soccer player named Vlado Kasalo was arrested as he prepared to fly home from Germany to Yugoslavia - he was accused of deliberately scoring own goals against his team, Nuremburg, to assist a Mafia-led betting racket.

The international defender was arrested in April 1991, and dismissed from his club after scoring the own goals in matches against Karlsruhe and Stuttgart.

Chapter VII

A Helping Hand

One outrageous conman who was caught in the full glare of the world's media spotlight, but nevertheless got away with his crime, was Maradona. Few England supporters will forget the day in June 1986 when 'Dirty Diego' punched the ball past England keeper Peter Shilton to give Argentina a 2-1 victory in a World Cup match.

Punters who had bet on the match to end as a draw were up in arms at being deprived of their winnings because of such a blatant piece of cheating.

Most soccer fans were also more than a little miffed that England had been knocked out of the World Cup in this manner.

Sympathising with both of these views, I came up with the idea of refunding stake money to all William Hill punters who had bet on the game to end in a draw - whilst also, of course, paying out to every one who had backed the official outcome to the game.

It cost William Hill over £10,000 in refunded stakes - but gained us probably a million pounds' worth of excellent publicity and goodwill - and, I am delighted to say, caused consternation amongst rival bookmakers, who sour-facedly rubbished the gesture and claimed it would set all kinds of precedents to take such an action!

Oddly enough, not one punter who received his or her money back was critical of the action, nor was the *Daily Mirror* which ran the story as its front page lead the day after the announcement was made.

C'est La Vie!

Whilst on the subject of Diego Maradona and his Argentinian con-men, let me tell you about the time in a previous World Cup - the 1978 one - that the Argentinians were the cause of my being accused of perpetrating a gambling con on the British nation by none other than Esther Rantzen.

However, in my defence I reckon that her attack on me and other bookies was as badly researched and as wide of the mark as the *Cook Report* on trainer Martin Pipe which caused such a furore in the racing world in mid 1991.

Still, to return to Ms Rantzen and her team, the gist of their complaint in *That's Life* on 2 July 1978 was that although Argentina had won the World Cup by beating Holland, according to William Hill they hadn't won the World Cup at all.

This confusion was simply caused by the long-standing football betting rule that when a bet is struck on the outcome of a match it refers to ninety minutes play - for betting purposes, extra time does not count.

As Argentina had actually won the World Cup by beating Holland 3-1 after extra time, in my opinion the *That's Life* mob decided to have a little fun at our expense - particularly as this rule had been in place for as long as anyone can remember, and still is to this day.

However, here is a transcript of the actual programme, showing how they tried to tie me up in knots.

Judge for yourself who was conning who:

ESTHER (RANTZEN): "Now we know you were hoping you'd heard the last about the World Cup, and we promise we won't mention it again, but there is just one thing we ought to tell you."

KIERAN (PRENDERVILLE): "Argentina did not win the World Cup."

ESTHER: "If you got it wrong, don't worry, quite a few newspapers got it wrong too."

GLYN (WORSNIP): "It's fiesta time as Argentina beat Holland 3-1; Argentina gained the first World Cup triumph; Argentina 3, Holland 1 - Daily Telegraph."

ESTHER: "Wrong, all wrong. Mr Maurice Stitt from Cleveleys in Lancashire wrote to tell us everyone had got it wrong. He said..."

KIERAN (Playing the punter): "I know, because I actually bet on the World Cup. I had a feeling in my bones that Argentina would win 3-1, so I went down to William Hills in Victoria Road, West Cleveley, and put £5 on it. When I watched the game on television I thought, 'bless my bones' and I started to plan what to do with all the money. On Monday I rushed back to William Hills, and the young lady smiled at me and said, 'You've won £95 sir, but I'll have to get the manager because I haven't got enough money in my drawer to pay you'. And so she went and got the manager and the manager came back and said, 'Sorry you lost'. 'Yes, I know, I'm going to buy my girlfriend a fur coat and have a slap up dinner for....what do you mean I lost?"

GLYN (Playing the manager): "I mean you lost, this is a losing bet."

KIERAN: "How can it be a losing bet, it says on the slip: World Cup Final, Argentina to win 3-1. Argentina won 3-1, give me my money."

GLYN: "Now, now, sir, it's an understandable mistake."

KIERAN: "It's not a mistake."

GLYN: "There, there, sir, it's just that you don't quite understand."

KIERAN: "What do you mean? I understand all right - I've just won £95; you've got it; I want it; hand it over."

GLYN: "Nothing would please me more, sir. It's just that football matches you see only last ninety minutes; anything after ninety minutes doesn't count."

KIERAN: "You'd better tell Argentina, they think they won. That's a good idea, why don't you go over there and tell them in person, they'll probably shoot you."

GLYN: "I think that's a little uncalled for, sir. Of course Argentina won the cup, but after ninety minutes it was 1-1 - no-one won; it was a draw; you lose, sorry."

ESTHER: "And there it was. Exactly the same thing happened to Mr Mike Heather. He put £6 on Argentina to win 3-1, with a betting shop called T. Benfield Sports Limited, in Kenton Road, Harrow. He told us..."

KIERAN (as Mr Heather): "I run a little off-licence, and when I realised I'd struck it rich I invited some friends over and we all had a slight celebration. That's why when I went round the next morning to collect my winnings, £116, and they said I'd won nothing, I thought I must be hearing things."

ESTHER: "Apparently he wasn't. The betting shop manager, Mr Young, explained to him..."

GLYN (as Mr Young): "You bet on the correct score. And the correct score after ninety minutes was 1-1. Sorry, that's the rules."

ESTHER: "Mr Heather went home, and thought about it, then he started to get rather angry. He told us..."

KIERAN: "Supposing I sold a bottle of Scotch which was really nothing but cold tea, could I just get away with it like that, if I put up a notice saying ALL BOTTLES WILL BE SOLD ACCORDING TO MY RULES, like the Benfield betting slips."

ESTHER: "It did seem rather unfair. We rang Benfields, and we spoke to Mr Young, and said: 'Why did Mr Heather lose?' Mr Young said..."

GLYN: "It's the rules and rules is rules."

ESTHER: "So we rang William Hills. We said Mr Stitt got it right, didn't he. The whole world seems to agree Argentina won the World Cup 3-1. Mr Sharpe told us..."

GLYN (Playing me): "No, Argentina drew 1-1 after 90 minutes play."

ESTHER: "But the game lasted 120 minutes and the score was 3-1."

GLYN: "You have to draw the line somewhere. The rule says 90 minutes."

ESTHER: "Well why don't you draw the line like the referees do at the end of the game? After all, who won the World Cup? "

GLYN: "Argentina."

ESTHER: "Who won their bets with you?"

GLYN: "The people who predicted that the World Cup would be a draw 1-1."

ESTHER: "So according to you, Argentina won the World Cup 1-1?"

GLYN: "Don't be silly."

ESTHER: "Well it did seem rather silly, so we rang and asked David Tench of the Consumers Association whether betting shops can just decide when a football match ends, and what the score is. He told us..."

KIERAN (Quoting Mr Tench): "If you have a legal contract with a betting shop, this might well be an unfair condition, so it would be illegal for them to impose their own rules like this. But betting is not a contract. Under the Gaming Act, it's a debt of honour, so if they say it was a draw, then it was a draw."

ESTHER: "That will certainly please our Dutch viewers. And there may be some other viewers who think they lost, because they bet on a 1-1 draw, so they'll be pleased too. According to today's paper, next week's Royal Commission on Gambling will suggest a large number of reforms. They might start by making a bet on the result mean the result of the match, not the result of the first 90 minutes."

There you are - and it is interesting to note that the Royal Commission did no such thing!

Follow, Follow The Smart Money

I'm pretty sure I was taken to the cleaners over a more recent soccer wager - but as it was over a bet which required punters to predict who would be the next manager of a big club it is hardly surprising.

My company is often asked to price up the potential candidates for the latest managerial vacancy. It is always a dodgy business as I am well aware that a great deal of behind the scenes wheeling and dealing goes on with a number of people in possession of certain significant information that the bookies are certainly not aware of.

So I was rather reluctant to offer odds about who would succeed Graeme Souness as boss of Glasgow Rangers, back in April 1991 - especially as a number of shrewd punters had already landed substantial bets by backing Souness to take over from Kenny Dalglish at Liverpool.

However, such was the interest in Scotland, where William Hill have a great many shops, that we duly opened a book, where it soon became obvious that what we had was the proverbial 'one-horse book'.

No-one wanted to back anyone other than Walter Smith, Souness's former right hand man. His odds plunged from 5-4 to 1-5 in the space of just three hours.

I knew we were being taken for a ride - and said so in the *Daily Record* of 18 April 1991, in which I was quoted as saying: "We are taking no more bets. Mr Smith is the only person anyone has wanted to back all day. We believe he has either been appointed already or soon will be."

The next day he was appointed - but not before I'd been woken in the middle of the night by a phone call from the Night News Editor of The Sun in Scotland telling me he was trying to get evidence to back up a story he wanted to run claiming that Rangers players and insiders had pulled off a massive coup by backing Walter Smith for the manager's job!

I told him we'd taken bets of up to £300, but that I had no idea who'd placed them and no way of ever finding out.

And I didn't lose too much sleep after he'd put the phone down. After all, that was part of the risk we were taking by ever opening the book.

But you won't be surprised to know that we didn't open a book a couple of months later when the Celtic job came up for grabs!

Chapter VIII

Touched Off On The Line

Racing was rocked by the Francasal affair in July 1953.

Santa Amaro and Francasal, both two-year-olds, were imported from France.

Santa Amaro was by far the better of the pair and ran in the name of Francasal in a selling race at Bath in July.

There was little money for the horse on the course, but off- course the cash piled on - over £6000 in total.

Bookmakers wishing to get in touch with the course to 'lay off' some of their liabilities discovered that the telephone lines were down - they had been deliberately cut.

'Francasal' won by two lengths at 10-1.

Five arrests were made in the September after the coup. The jury failed to agree at the end of the first trial and a second was held, after which there were four convictions, the longest sentence being three years.

Evidence from a farrier, a vet, a transporter and trainers eventually produced the proof of the switch of horses and all bets on the race were declared void.

The Big Sting

Probably the most startling attempted coup on the French turf occurred in 1973 when nine outsiders were inexplicably heavily backed for the Tierce (a first, second and third forecast bet) in the Prix Bride Abattue at Auteuil.

So heavy and unexpected was the betting that the authorities were alerted and were watching closely as the race began.

After less than a quarter of a mile, the field of 24 had split into two - with the nine backed horses heading the rest. Eventually the first three went past the post, all outsiders, all amongst the suspiciously backed nine - and paying a dividend of over 13,500 francs to a three franc stake.

The authorities immediately refused to pay out. Investigations began, but took an incredible five years to complete - at which stage an amazing FOURTEEN jockeys and FORTY punters were arrested for conspiracy to defraud the public.

Mist A Circuit

The dense fog surrounding Delta Downs, Louisiana racecourse, in January 1990, gave jockey Sylvester Carmouche an idea as the runners came under orders for the race in which he was about to ride 23-1 outsider Landing Officer in January 1990.

As the field set off, Carmouche allowed the rest of the runners to disappear off into the mist. He, meanwhile, reined his horse in shortly after the start and waited in the fog until the other runners returned to set off on their second circuit.

At this stage, Carmouche produced the fresh Landing Officer, which promptly stormed home twenty five lengths clear of the pack!

Carmouche got his come-uppance though - twice.

Firstly he was suspended for ten years by the Lousiana Racing Commission.

Then he was taken to trial by State Prosecutors for the attempted theft of 90 dollars - the difference between the 140 dollars he would have been paid had his victory been upheld and the 50 dollar normal riding fee.

He was convicted of attempted theft and ordered to spend thirty days in jail.

After the trial, Carmouche, who claimed he hadn't been spotted in the race because he had kept to the far side of the course, commented in a Southern drawl, "It ain't right. I know I ain't did it."

Turning The Tables

Villainous Yorkshire crook and conman Robert Ridsdale bribed jockey Harry Edwards to stop Jerry, a hot fancy for the 1824 St Leger. He then accepted huge bets for the horse, safe in the knowledge that it could not win.

On the eve of the race, Jerry's trainer got wind of Ridsdale's activities.

The next afternoon, just as Edwards appeared clad in his racing colours and ready for the race, the trainer informed him his services were no longer required and substituted him with trustworthy jockey Ben Smith, who went out and rode the horse to victory.

Weighed In

An inebriated punter who tried to win himself a few quid whilst waiting for a train back to London after the 1991 Cheltenham Festival was instead taken to the cleaners.

He had, reported the *Sunday Times*, hit on the idea of standing next to the weighing machine on the platform of Evesham Station and offering odds about how much various people weighed.

"A crowd soon gathered and serious money began to change

hands," reported the Sunday Times, revealing what happened next:
"Enter the City sting merchants. Here was an opportunity for lucrative insider dealing and an unlikely trio swooped to make a killing. The threesome - a leading PR man, a stockbroker and a leggy City hackette with an Australian accent were spotted whispering in the corner. Soon the hackette, who reports on fraud, was standing on the scales while her accomplices estimated her weight. They 'guessed' 62 kilos and surprise, surprise, that was precisely how much little Miss Innocent weighed. The distressed odds maker coughed up £40 and the coup was complete."

Clearly a case of the three cad trick!

Radio Won

Jockey Scobie Breasley drove a moderate horse called Buoyancy home to a 6-1 victory in the 7½ furlong Berkeley Welter at Ascot, Melbourne, in December 1939. But even as he was taking the horse into the winners enclosure, radio listeners were still hearing a race they believed had yet to finish!

For the race was the subject of a cleverly organised plot which involved cutting the radio broadcast cables of every station connected up to the track, except for one - Radio Station 3XY of Melbourne.

The links were cut just as the horses leapt into action.

At this point agents involved in the coup were avidly listening to Radio 3XY where an already agreed code was being used to advise those 'in the know' about which horse had won the race.

Once the race had finished in reality, so Radio 3XY began a 'phantom' broadcast of a race which had already finished!

Of course the plotters were all on a 'certainty' and, once the phantom broadcast had finished, they rushed to be paid out.

But meanwhile a major flaw in the plot had emerged. One of the stations had been left in communication with the track just too long, and listeners had heard commentary on the early stages of the race.

The word soon spread as news of the cut cables became known and suspicious bookies refused to pay, while radio station bosses launched an instant investigation.

Radio Station 3XY commentator Harry Solomons was sacked within an hour - and he ended up in jail for fraud.

Even so, the coup was believed to have netted some £20,000 before the pay out block went on.

Shocks Galore

An owner was warned off for five years when a battery-powered riding boot was discovered by officials of the Brisbane Turf Club in 1928 and there have been a number of well documented instances of batteries being used in an effort to shock horses into greater efforts.

In 1955, at Adelaide, there was a massive plunge on a horse called Thundering Legion, which was backed down from 33-1 to 7-2 shortly before the race.

Suspicious stewards removed intended jockey Bill Attrill from the horse after discovering he was carrying a battery powered whip.

The horse was allowed to ride with a substitute jockey on board - and, amazingly, stormed to victory, thus fairly landing all those crookedly inspired wagers!

However, Attrill was later disqualified for ten years and the trainer, N.Conway, for life - although this was later reduced to ten years.

Batteries have been concealed in saddles, lead bags, various items of equipment and clothing. They can be dangerous, potentially fatal if misused, causing a horse to act unpredictably and possibly to fall.

Good Guestwork

American owner Raymond Guest was socialising with a bookmaker, the late William Hill, when he asked Hill what price he would offer about a two-year-old colt he had winning the 1968 Derby.

Mr Hill offered a bet of £500 each way at odds of 100-1.

The horse was Sir Ivor, which won the 1968 Derby at odds of 4-5, winning Mr Guest £62,500 from William Hill for that inspired wager.

No, No, After You

Bookmaker George Hodgman and three of his friends were financially embarrassed late in 1862, so they devised a fool-proof plan to make some money.

Hodgman arranged for the running of a new race, the Welter Handicap at Shrewsbury, keeping details of the event secret for as long as possible in the hope that the four horses he had entered under various owners' names would be the only entries.

Unfortunately, though, someone else heard about the event - a Mr Priestley, who decided to enter his horse, Tom Sayers.

Hodgman and his pals decided they would let Tom Sayers win - so they duly informed their jockeys that they were not expected to win and arranged to stake £1000 on Tom Sayers.

Tom Sayers's jockey, George Fordham, was unaware of the coup, so was rather surprised, firstly, to notice that his horse, with no worthwhile form to his credit, was backed down to Even money favourite, and secondly that when Tom Sayers whipped round at the start of the race, all the other jockeys brought their horses back and insisted on a restart!

Once they finally got underway, the other jockeys made it their business to take their time about completing the course - while Tom Sayers, running a genuine race, was able to win by three quarters of a length.

The plotters collected £2500 for their efforts - and Fordham was said to be greatly amused when eventually acquainted with the circumstances of the race.

Chinese Whispers

Hong Kong jockey Tse Wai-ho admitted to a court in March 1991 that he had been supplied with a schoolgirl and a British prostitute for sex, in return for racing tips given to local police officers.

A Bright Future

A cunningly schemed plot almost landed a £300,000 touch for its perpetrators, when a horse called Gay Future won at Cartmel on August Bank Holiday Monday, 1974.

Troon permit trainer Anthony Collins had four horses due to run on the day - Gay Future and Racionzer at Cartmel, Opera Cloak at Southwell and Ankerwyke at Plumpton.

On the morning of the race a group of people set off to place some £30,000 worth of bets on Gay Future - mainly in £5, £10 or £15 doubles with either Opera Cloak or Ankerwyke.

This was a very shrewd move as bookmakers are normally only suspicious when horses are backed singly and less likely to pay much attention to bets which involve more than one selection.

However, the sheer volume of bets being placed eventually alerted the bookies, with William Hill refusing to accept any more bets involving Gay Future or the other two, shortly after mid-day.

Collins himself was at Plumpton, ostensibly to look after Ankerwyke, while his wife had gone to Cartmel to look after Gay Future and, importantly, to place on-course bets on Collins's other entry in the same race, Racionzer, clearly to give the impression that this was the fancied horse of the two, and to keep the price for Gay Future higher than it might otherwise have been.

Further parts of the plot began to fit into place - the unknown amateur who had been declared as Gay Future's jockey was suddenly replaced by leading Irish amateur Mr T.A.Jones, who had ridden Gay Future to victory in Ireland before.

Before Gay Future entered the parade ring, soap flakes were rubbed into his flanks - making it look like he was sweating up.

The bookies, aware that something was amiss but not sure what, had sent representatives to each of the courses at which Collins had entered runners.

The men who reached Plumpton and Southwell were baffled to discover that both Opera Cloak and Ankerwyke had been withdrawn from their races.

Cartmel being somewhat remote, the bookies' man sent there failed to arrive on time. Gay Future, making his debut over hurdles, sauntered in by fifteen lengths at odds of 10-1!

The Betting Office Licencees Association, to which most of the leading off-course bookmakers in the UK belong, advised members to withhold payment of bets on Gay Future, pending the outcome of enquiries into the case.

Many smaller companies paid out regardless, but major companies decided to wait - Ladbrokes withheld a reported £10,180, Mecca £14,946, Hills £5322 and Coral £4056.

BOLA called in Scotland Yard to investigate. Eventually the Police took the decision to prosecute. Collins and Irish building contractor William Murphy appeared at Preston Crown Court in mid February 1976, charged with conspiracy to defraud bookmakers.

After a seven day trial both were found guilty, fined £1000 and ordered to pay £500 towards prosecution costs.

The judge commented: "On the facts of the case, the degree of dishonesty is in my assessment, although a conspiracy to defraud, very much at the bottom end of the scale."

Following the case the Sporting Life ruled that all bets on the race won by Gay Future were void. BOLA advised members to return stakes and, after a six month period, to donate any unclaimed to a racing charity.

The main point brought out by the prosecution during the case was that the conspirators had never intended for Opera Cloak or Ankerwyke to take part in the races for which they had been entered - this was just a subterfuge to enable them to back Gay Future without drawing attention to the fact.

There was also much discussion about whether the rule that, before a trainer could run a horse under Jockey Club rules, the horse had to have been under the care of licensed trainers or permit holders in this country for at least 28 days, or to have been trained by qualified trainers in its country of origin, had been broken.

A horse arrived from Dublin at Collins's Troon, Ayrshire stables on 29 July 1974, with the initials G.F. on its coat. However, it was alleged this horse was actually an unnamed gelding, while Gay Future was really still in Ireland being prepared by a well known trainer for the Cartmel coup and that the real Gay Future was only shipped over to Liverpool two days before the race and driven straight to the racecourse stables at Cartmel.

Whatever the whys and wherefores of the case - and it should be reiterated that it was the Police and not the bookmakers who decided to prosecute - Gay Future himself enjoyed no happy ending; he suffered a fatal fall during a hurdle race at Wetherby three weeks before the Preston trial.

Doping Scandals

The most recent example of a serious doping incident took place during the St Leger meeting at Doncaster in 1990, and at the time of going to press was still unsolved.

Bravefoot, who finished last in the Champagne Stakes, and Norwich, fourth in the Kiveton Park Stakes, were both found to have been doped.

The following week, Flying Diva, last of three in the Norfolk Stakes at Yarmouth, was also tested positive.

All three horses were found to have been administered a sedative, Acetylpromazine (ACP), and were believed to have been given the substance within racecourse stables.

Andrew Parker Bowles, Jockey Club steward responsible for racecourses, confirmed that since these incidents racecourse stable security had been stepped up. "We realised things had gone wrong at Doncaster and Yarmouth," he told the media, "but before then we had had a period of about twenty years when there had been no evidence of any doping."

Blowing In The Wind

A winning betting slip worth £7300 blew off the balcony belonging to a 22-year-old Frenchman who had written a thesis on gambling to get his degree.

But when Ronald Simon decided to try to collect on the slip from a Worcester Park, Surrey betting shop he found himself arrested and charged with attempted deception - and with a £500 fine and a nine month suspended jail sentence hanging over his head.

Dog-gone

In August 1978, the Daily Mirror reported that a group of London greyhound followers had hit on a smart scheme - enter ALL the dogs in an open race up north, then clean up by backing the one they knew to be the best dog.

So they entered five greyhounds for a race at Askern Stadium, near Doncaster and five carloads of them drove up to pull off the coup, only to discover when they arrived that it wasn't a FIVE dog race - there was a sixth entry, local dog Reggie.

But, with Reggie badly drawn, the Londoners went ahead with their betting plunge, only for 'sod's law' to strike as Reggie stormed home by seven lengths.

A spokesman for the track, Graham Searson, was quoted as saying: "As soon as they entered their five dogs we warned the bookies, but two were prepared to take bets.

All the locals thought it was a great laugh when Reggie won - the Cockneys certainly went home with their tails between their legs."

Down The Pan

Kenneth Bleach's ingenious bid to 'lick' the bookies came unstuck in 1971. The Oldham lorry driver came up with his scheme after being supplied with addressed envelopes by Postal Turf Services Ltd, with whom he had an account.

Bleach wrote his own address on a slip on paper, gummed it over the firm's name and sent the letter to himself, removing the paper with his address on when he received it back.

He then drove from Oldham to Epsom, where Postal Turf Services had their offices, and 'posted' his envelope - in which he had now inserted a 'winning' betting slip - through the door.

Faultless? Well, it may have been, but for the suspicious post office worker who spotted the bookie's address under the gummed, self-addressed piece of paper and alerted officials.

The only thing Bleach won in the end was a 12-month suspended jail sentence.

Stewards Inquiry?

The extraordinary phenomenon of no horse managing to finish the course in an apparently straightforward flat race is probably unprecedented.

But a race took place at Marsi in Malta in February 1969, in which there were three 'runners' but apparently no 'triers'.

Connections weren't talking, but the assumption was that not one of the horses involved in the race was 'off' that day.

The race was supposed to be a sprint but with very little of the race still to run, and the three horses neck and neck, Tetchy suddenly slowed to a halt and his jockey dismounted.

Almost immediately Malus did likewise, leaving Plaster Saint cruising to victory - until with yards to go, the horse veered to one side and his jockey also dismounted.

All three horses were led over the finishing line by their reins and the race was declared a 'no race', all stakes being returned.

All three jockeys had their licences withdrawn. All three owners were warned off.

Blank Check

Bookie Hector MacDonald was approached by a punter wishing to place a bet of £1000 cash to win £1750 on Vital Season at Epsom in September 1979.

The punter handed over a sealed packet of £20 notes and MacDonald put them in his pocket - a few minutes later, trusting soul though he felt himself to be, MacDonald decided to count the cash.

There was £40 there - two genuine £20 notes, separated by a thick wad of blank sheets of paper!

The ring inspector arrived and promptly agreed that the bet should be reduced to one of £40.

Doubling Up

The settler in a Liverpool betting shop was staggered when a bet, placed and timed at 1.40pm and with the name of a horse just about to run written on it, suddenly began to change before her very eyes!

Another horse's name, along with the word 'double' was beginning to appear on the slip and - surprise, surprise - it was the name of a horse which had ALREADY won earlier in the day, at long odds.

The additional words had been added in invisible ink, which slowly became visible over a period of time and, of course, assuming the other horse on the slip was a winner, the punter stood to con his way to a substantial win bonus.

However, when he did call to collect his winnings he found a welcoming committee consisting of a couple of burly constables waiting to escort him off the premises.

Chapter IX

Tender A Resignation

I should hate to have to take the blame for Margaret Thatcher deciding to step down as Prime Minister - but there is persuasive evidence, revealed here for the first time, which suggests she did it for fear of being accused of pulling off a gambling coup!

Now, I hope I don't draw the attention of MI5 in my direction for what I am about to exclusively reveal - so don't tell them, will you?

Anyway, it all began when I decided that Mrs T might well be interested to know I had opened up a book on the likelihood or otherwise of the pound sterling still being legal tender in the UK by 1 January of the year 2000.

I wrote to her during the Autumn of 1990, when the great debate was raging about whether the Ecu would eventually become the UK's legal tender.

Mrs Thatcher replied to me, via her Private Secretary Barry Potter, on 1 November 1990, expressing her interest in the fact that the odds were available, but drawing attention to the fact that for her to avail herself of the odds might well lead to accusations of insider trading.

Said the letter from Number Ten: "I am sure that the Prime Minister will be interested to know the odds on offer. You will appreciate, however, that it is most unlikely that the Prime Minister will wish to avail herself of this facility: the dangers of 'insider trading' are all too clear."

Shortly after I received this letter, Mrs Thatcher took her momentous decision to quit as Prime Minister!

I can only surmise that the threat of these insider trading charges had weighed so heavily on her mind since my letter, she had decided the only way to ensure her honour remained unimpugned, and her reputation free of a gambling scandal, was to resign.

It is a humbling feeling to realise that one has played a key role in an event of international significance such as this, and to reflect that but for my decision to bet on the Ecu issue, Mrs T might still have been in power to this day.

Shergar and Spice

My favourite holiday destination has long been Jersey - even before Bergerac popularised the island - but during my time there I had

10 DOWNING STREET
LONDON SW1A 2AA

From the Private Secretary

1 November 1990

Dear Mr Sharpe,

Thank you for your letter of 31 October indicating the odds which William Hill are prepared to offer that the pound sterling will still be legal tender in the UK on 1 January 2000.

I am sure that the Prime Minister will be interested to know the odds on offer. You will appreciate, however, that it is most unlikely that the Prime Minister will wish to avail herself of this facility: the dangers of "insider trading" are all too clear.

Yours sincerely,

Barry Potts

Barry Potter

Graham Sharpe, Esq.

never previously dreamed that the green fields of the nine miles by five resort might be harbouring the answer to one of the turf's enduring mysteries - what became of Shergar!

So I was mildly astonished one day in late March 1991, when a contact of mine, who writes for The Sun, rang me to ask what I'd say if he told me he knew where Shergar had been since the infamous kidnap incident in 1983.

"I'd say you'd had a good lunch," I replied.

But he was deadly serious and he told me he'd got wind of a story that a group of bounty hunters were seeking a third of a million pounds finder's fee for revealing to insurance chiefs that Shergar was alive and well and grazing in a field in Jersey!

Well, coincidentally, I had watched the Jersey Derby at the local course, Les Landes, when I'd been there the previous summer, but I was pretty sure the winner hadn't been Shergar.

I told my contact that in betting terms it was a 10,000-1 shot that there was anything in the story, and it was odds-on that the claim was a mega-con.

Sure enough, though, the next day's Sun (28 March 1991) ran as its lead story the headline, 'Shergar Is Alive'.

As soon as the paper hit the newstands, my phone started ringing - it was the producers of radio programmes who wanted to run interviews with me about whether I believed there was anything in the story.

At 8am I was standing in my hallway chatting to Angela Rippon on London's LBC Radio about Shergar and Jersey. Another broadcaster told me he had just been talking to racing expert Derek Thompson about the story, to which I replied: "I'd disregard anything Derek tells you as he once wrote a story in The Sport in which he claimed to have seen Lord Lucan at York racecourse!"

The Sun quoted Steve Chappell, deputy chairman of Lloyds Bloodstock Committee, as confirming that a middle-man had tried to negotiate a £365,000 finder's fee.

Said Chappell: "We have been informed Shergar is alive, but we have no concrete proof and I am very sceptical. It would seem someone is trying to negotiate a payment, but I have made it clear that Lloyds will never pay a finder's fee or ransom for the return of any stolen horse."

According to the middle man, continued the story, the kidnappers of Shergar took the horse to the Middle East to sell him back to his owner, the Aga Khan, but when the Aga refused to pay, he was switched to the Channel Islands.

Various experts and people involved with the case poured scorn to the claims and my contact at The Sun told me he was convinced this had been an attempted con - although how the bounty hunters had intended to convince anyone they genuinely had the horse remains a mystery.

Assuming they had been believed, they would have had to produce a horse which at least LOOKED like Shergar, some eight years on - but they were probably frightened off by the sudden publicity.

I should imagine the riding stables in Jersey and Guernsey were delighted by all the fuss, though - how many tourists would be looking to go riding during their holidays, and then return home to dine out on the story of 'how I rode Shergar around the Channel Islands'!

All Weather Betting

Betting on the weather has become increasingly popular in this country ever since I took out a commercial contract with the London Weather Centre under the terms of which they will supply me with statistics and information so that I can offer people the opportunity of betting on their own weather forecasts.

One of these amateur Met-men - Gabe Roberts from Ashford Kent - pulled off a £14,000 coup a year or two back by betting that the UK would have one of its warmest autumns ever - it did and the punter duly collected.

Another regular big money meteorological punter is Piers Corbyn, brother of Labour MP Jeremy, and an astrophycisist. Piers bets over £600 per month with me on what the weather will get up to, and he is so successful that his profits are now in the four figure bracket. He has launched a commercial forecasting business of his own on the back of this success - rightly claiming in his publicity that he is the only weather-man willing to put his money where his meteorological mouth is!

Piers's biggest coup was in successfully forecasting the high winds which battered the country for two winters in succession, but despite his winning wagers he has yet to convince my advisers at the London Weather Centre that his predictions are any more accurate than their's - despite my teasing comments to Bob Aran and his Met Office colleagues that perhaps THEY should start betting with me and I should employ Piers to advise me on the odds.

Weather betting is big business now. Peter Bromage-Smith, a London businessman, bet £1000 on a white Christmas a year or two ago and in July 1991 an attractive young lady walked into a Blackpool betting shop and handed over £1000 in £50 notes to bet that the temperature in the UK would reach 100F at some time during the summer of that year, at odds of 12-1.

The woman had only ever been seen in the shop on one previous occasion - when she backed a 25-1 Royal Ascot winner and won £1257! She must have had a 'hot tip' about the weather bet.

The previous year, 1990, had seen many weather punters backing a warm 'un as I offered the over-generous odds of 100-1 about the UK's current record temperature being exceeded - it was, on 3 August 1990 when the guage hit 98.8F.

Sweating Over A Result

I had to allow weather punters to 'con' us out of up to £25,000 in July 1991 when the inaccuracy of certain newspapers left me literally hot under the collar.

At the beginning of that month I'd offered 5-1 about the temperature anywhere in the UK hitting 90F. It proved to be a popular offer and plenty of bets were struck, with the odds plummeting down to evens, at which point we decided to close the book.

On Thursday 11 July a mini-heatwave arrived in the UK and I started to sweat on the bet being won.

I checked hourly with the Met Office to discover just how hot it was getting. They told me Cromer in Norfolk was out in front, but that the temperature looked like stalling at 32.1C, just under 90F.

So imagine my surprise to read the papers the next day and see that the Daily Telegraph, on its front page, was reporting that the temperature in Cromer had hit 90F.

Upon investigation, I learned the 32.1C quoted to me the previous day was, in fact, correct - and translated to 89.8F, a figure accurately reported by, amongst others, the Daily Mail and the Sun.

However, for reasons best known to themselves, the Weather Centre and certain papers had decided to 'round' the figure up and quote it as 90F.

Of course, once the punters saw that such a reliable journal as the Telegraph was happy 90F had been reached, they wanted paying - and, as it would have caused such confusion to have argued against it, we decided we'd better pay up and look happy!

It wasn't too easy to look happy, though, particularly when two of the recipients of our largesse were reporters working for one of the papers which had reported the 90F - not, it must be pointed out, the Telegraph.

Still, I got some revenge on the Weather Centre's Commercial Manager Bob Aran, who had invited my wife and I to the Regents Park Open Air Theatre to see a performance of Macbeth the very next evening.

With ominous clouds threatening to produce a deluge of rain on the heads of the audience and excellent New Shakespeare Company actors, I promised Bob that if it rained I would immediately get on to my tabloid contacts to sell them a story along the lines of 'Weathermen's Open Air Outing Rained Off'.

An anxious Bob spent as much time watching the sky as he did the superb production!

Rain Check

And in June 1991, I nearly made another 100-1 blunder to give punters pennies from heaven and William Hill a soaking.

I'd casually quoted 100-1 when asked for odds that rain would fall in London every single day of any calendar month.

So I wasn't too worried when it poured for the first week of June. However, as a precaution I cut the odds to 50-1 and put out a little publicity story to that effect.

It rained for the whole of the second week. Down came the odds again - to 20-1 - with our liabilities escalating rapidly as bets of up to £100 were taken.

By the time it had rained throughout the third week the odds were down to 5-1, the liabilities were adding up to serious money and I was thinking about hiring a Red Indian Chief to do the opposite of the rain-dance in my office.

At the end of the third week, the Wimbledon tournament started, so I thought 'in for a penny, in for a pound' and offered 100-1 about rain interrupting play on the Centre Court on every day of the Tournament fortnight.

Come 28 June, there were just two days to go. It had rained every single day of the month in London and the forecast was showers for the next two days. I cut the odds down to 4-6. Meanwhile, rain had interrupted play on the Centre Court for the first five days of play and the odds about it doing so every day were down to 8-1.

Our liabilities on both had reached £50,000. I'd even had the Managing Director on the phone enquiring politely what the bloody hell I thought I was up to giving money away on the damned rain!

Saturday 29 June 1991 dawned warm and sunny - but forecasters were still tipping showers for late in the day.

It stayed dry all morning. And all afternoon.

In the evening I went to the races at Lingfield. People kept coming up to me and pointing out rain clouds in the distance. "Looks like rain in London," they crowed.

I backed one horse all night. It was a namesake - Sharp Chief. The race was a sprint. Sharp Chief finished tailed off. My luck was not in.

Unable to take the pressure any longer I spent the last two hours of the day in an Indian restaurant in Lingfield trying not to look outside at what the weather was doing. Inside, I, at least, was pouring - wine!

Shortly after midnight on the last day of the calendar month a nervous phone call to the resident forecaster at the Weather Centre brought the good news I'd been praying for: "There hasn't been a drop of rain all day."

Within a couple of hours the heavens opened and rain poured down. But it was too late - we'd avoided that soaking!

Party Whip?

Let me take this opportunity to reassure my wife, Sheila, that my relationship with Ms Lindi 'Whiplash' St-Claire is conducted purely on a business basis - my business, that is, not her's!

Lindi, a charming lady, one of whose paying pastimes seems to be tying people up and submitting them to physical and mental torture - for which they appear to be only too happy to cough up - is also a frequent user of my services - betting wise.

For Lindi is the leader of the Corrective Party, one of whose first actions upon coming to power would be to legalise prostitution.

What has all this got to do with betting, I hear you ask?

Well, Lindi, whose regular Valentine and Christmas cards advertising her Miss Whiplash activities first aroused my wife's suspicions, is constantly on the look-out for a spectacular betting coup.

At by-elections, she has bet on her chances, which are, she admits, slim to say the least. But she holds out far more hopes for her infant twins, whom she firmly believes are destined for political glories.

She has taken odds of 2039-1 with me that either of them, Kenneth or Kennella, will have been elected to Parliament by the time they are fifty years old - and the reason for those strange odds is that 2039 is the year they will have to be elected by to land the bet.

While waiting for that particular wager to pay off, Lindi has also backed herself to become the first Madam to open a brothel on the Moon, Mars, Venus or any other planet before the year 2010! That's the bet she asked for. I actually gave her odds of 10,000-1 about setting foot on the moon - what she gets up to once she's there is her business!

Lindi is also happy to invest a few bob about her chances of, "marrying into one of the world's Royal families and becoming the wife of either a prince, a king, an emperor or a sultan, within four years."

Yes, I'd have thought the twins might have put a small obstacle in the way of that one, too - but with the number of Royals there seem to be all over the place these days I reckon she's probably on an odds-on shot!

Graham sharp.
William Hill.
Press office.   November 8th, 1989.
19, Valentine Place.
SE18QH.

Dear Graham,

Hello there, here I am again for another whacky bet.

I bet that my twins who were born on August 6th 1989
will become M.P.'s at the British House of Parliament by
the time they are 50 yrs of age (say the year 2040).
There names are Kenneth Jefferson Tory Lindon (the boy)
and Kenella Mexico Tahiti Lindi (the girl).

I note that you are prepared to offer odds of 2039 to 1
for this particular bet and therefore I would like to bet
£25 for each child.PLUS TAX.

I enclose my cheque in the sum of £55.

ALSO, further to my existing that I will walk on the
surface of the Moon at odds of 10,000-1. I would be keen
to hear what odds you could offer on the undermentioned
bets?

1. I bet that I will step foot on ANY planet in outer
space by 2010.

2. I bet that I will be the first Human female to 'mate'
with a non-Human Alien.

3. I bet that I will give birth to the first
interplanetary child as a result of mating with a
non-Human Alien male from another planet/star/moon/galaxy
or solar system etc.

I look forward to hearing from you in due course.

Thank you,

Best wishes,

Chapter X

Like It Or Lump It

A scam pulled in the late forties by one racket boss against another, in the States, brought a whole new meaning to the term fly-boy.

Willie Moretti and Bugsy Siegel were inveterate gamblers. One day the pair were together in a hotel.

Bugsy invited Moretti to take breakfast with him.

The breakfast order Bugsy made was a little unusual - he concluded it by asking Room Service: "Send up a dozen live flies."

Moretti was dumbfounded when the waiter arrived with the breakfast on a serving tray and a small, ventilated, buzzing box.

"Willie," said Bugsy, "I know you're a gambler, and I've come across a game which beats Poker, Craps or any other betting game. It's a Spanish game called La Mosca."

Bugsy took two lumps of sugar from the tray and placed them on the coffee table about six inches apart.

"The idea of the game is to guess which lump of sugar the first fly will land on. For five grand."

Still slightly suspicious, Moretti asked whether Bugsy had trained the flies in some way. "Are you joking - besides, you heard me order them."

The bet was made, the flies released and a minute or two later one landed on the lump nominated by Bugsy.

Convinced by now that he had been had, Moretti demanded the right to choose first this time.

Bugsy agreed and adding, "And we'll move the lumps a little further apart, too", pushed one a few inches further along.

Seconds later - zoom, down came the fly - straight on to Bugsy's cube.

Moretti had lost ten grand.

Later he discovered that Bugsy had 'gaffed' the sugar with a tiny drop of DDT on one side of each lump. He'd left the 'gaffed' side upwards until the lumps had been chosen, then he had surreptitiously moved the lumps and turned his one over.

Marx Cards

It must have been one of the most crooked games of Gin Rummy ever when Chicago mob leader Johnny Roselli and his unscrupulous accomplices took on noted crooked gambler and comedian Zeppo Marx along with his team of Hollywood stars, including Phil 'Bilko' Silvers.

The game took place in 1968 at the Beverly Hills Friars Club - and when it was over the Roselli team was $400,000 the richer.

Mind you, luck and skill had probably played little part in the game - the Chicago team having hired an electronics expert to install cheating devices. One of the players, working at a peephole in the ceiling, was signalling information to one of the players at the table who was wearing concealed devices about his person.

Not that the Marx squad were completely innocent, however; Zeppo, like his brother Chico, had a reputation for having perfected elaborate signalling methods to turn the odds in his favour.

Marx was not noted as a good loser, though, and the Roselli squad was eventually convicted of swindling the stars.

Taking The Proverbial!

Sprinter Major Leon was drug tested after winning a race in Victoria, Australia in 1969.

Imagine the reaction when it was revealed that the urine sample taken from the horse was 'of human origin'!

Connections of the horse were subsequently fined for 'improper practices'.

Original Sin

Crooked gambling goes back as far as gambling itself. That's the conclusion reached by Carl Sifakis, author of American book The *Encyclopaedia of Gambling* (Facts On File), who, in his introduction to the book explains:

"Who came first in the history of man, the gambler or the cheater? The conventional wisdom is that early man came up with gambling as a form of sport or play.

However, nothing unearthed by archaeologists is inconsistent with the flip side of the argument, that prehistoric cheaters actually invented gambling as a method of getting something from their fellow man.

The earliest form of primitive dice, dating by various estimates from 6000 to 3500BC, turns out to be crooked dice.

It should be emphasised that dice appear in all cultures in vastly separate areas of the globe and developed in the same basic form, always with cheating pieces amongst the earliest types found."

Read All About Me

Surely Bernard Murphy is the only man who has ever used a gambling coup to win an election!

In 1985, Murphy was contesting a council election in Cork City, Ireland, when he and his assistant, John Lennon (really!), noticed the local bookmaker, Liam Cashman, was quoting him at 33-1 to be elected.

Murphy and Lennon promptly printed and distributed posters and pamphlets pointing out to the local populace that here was a great chance to "vote yourself money" by backing Murphy and then voting for him.

Suddenly, no-hoper Murphy, sometime newspaper vendor and sandwich board-man, became a talking point. Cashman was forced to slash his odds from 33-1 to 9-4 and acquired a £20,000 liability in the process.

Independent candidate Murphy, one of whose major policy points was the abolition of gas meters, polled over 1000 votes and won the seat!

Liam Cashman declined a request to quote odds about Murphy being elected to Parliament.

Misplaced Loyalty

The filly Blink Bonny won both the Derby and the Oaks in 1857 and, unsurprisingly, was a short priced favourite for the St Leger. However, unscrupulous bookmaker John Jackson bribed the filly's jockey, Charlton, who had ridden her in both big race triumphs, to pull the horse.

Only the presence of prize-fighter Tom Sayers saved Blink Bonny's owner, William I'Anson, from a severe beating at the hands of the Doncaster crowd when the horse returned after the race.

Jackson had heavily backed the winner, Imperieuse, a 100-6 shot, and fielded against the favourite Blink Bonny.

I'Anson had actually been informed in advance of the plot but had decided, misguidedly, to stand by his jockey and trust to his loyalty.

A Tricky Customer

Alvin Clarence Thomas, better known as 'Titanic' Thompson, born in 1892, became a legendary gambler - but from an early age, he liked to have the odds on his side.

At the age of just six he pulled his first 'sting' at a fishing hole near his home where he would go with his spaniel, Carlo.

When a passer-by admired the dog, the youngster explained that this was a very smart dog - he could dive to the bottom of the fishing hole and retrieve any stone you threw down there.

The passer-by found this unlikely, so the boy offered to wager the dog against the passer-by's fishing rod.

The passer-by duly selected a stone, which the boy marked with an 'x'. The passer-by threw it in, the dog jumped in after it and soon reappeared with a stone in its mouth - incredibly the stone was marked with an 'x'.

The passer-by handed over the rod.

Said Titanic, some years later: "That dog of mine was good at that trick. He was very good. But I ain't one for taking chances. A few days before, I'd covered the bottom of that hole with dozens of rocks marked with an 'x'."

One night, Thompson deliberately moved a signpost saying 'Joplin - 20 miles' some five miles nearer the town. The next day, driving along with some fellow gamblers, he bet them the sign was wrong!

On yet another occasion he went to the trouble of stopping a lorry carrying a wagonload of water melons and offered to buy the lot - on condition that the driver counted them and then agreed to drive the lorry through the centre of town, past a local hotel, a favourite haunt of gamblers, at a given time.

Thompson just happened to suggest a wager on how many melons the lorry was carrying!

Other famous strokes he pulled included winning walnut-throwing wagers by using a walnut filled with lead, and taking on golfers whom he had lost to when playing right handed, but this time playing left handed. Only afterwards did the suckers discover that he was a left-hander who had taught himself to play fairly well right handed.

Havana Bad Time

The arguments amongst boxing purists rage until this day - was the 1915 heavyweight title fight between Jack Johnson and Jess Willard in Havana, Cuba, crooked?

Boxing fans, arguing that to a man of Johnson's ability the shame of losing his title to a journeyman like Willard - even at the admittedly ancient age of 37 - would have been too much to take, cannot accept that Johnson threw the fight on behalf of gambling crooks.

Gamblers, on the other hand, reason that every man has his price and note the fact that far more money than would otherwise have been expected was wagered on the outsider - including a significantly large amount by a good friend of Johnson, the gambler Wilson Mizner.

Mizner, reportedly, heard rumours that all was not well with the conduct of the fight, so took the precaution of contacting his friend Johnson via a wire, asking him: "What shall I do?"

Receiving no reply, Mizner reasoned the fight must be bent and bet thousands of dollars on Willard, who duly took a pasting early on, only to come through to win by a knockout in Round 26.

Luck Of The Draw

The story is told of William Jones, known as 'Canada Bill', an Englishman who emigrated to Canada in the mid 19th century, where he proceeded to amass a fortune by swindling the naive Canadians by means of the three card trick, which he worked on railway trains.

Having made a crooked pile he was, it is reported, moved to stake $180,000 on an honest gamble - the draw of a card.

As one would suspect from such a morality tale, he duly lost the draw - and with it the bulk of his fortune, which he was never to replenish, heading downhill at a rapid rate following this setback and eventually dying in poverty.

Dead Cert?

It was surely the ultimate compliment to him that at his funeral an acquaintance offered to wager $1000 to $500 "that Bill is not in the box".

Such was the reputation of the hustler that the bet found no takers - indeed another mourner commented that he had, "known Bill to squeeze through tighter holes than that!"

All's Well That Ends Wells

They wrote a song about what he did. He became a popular hero.

But 'The Man Who Broke The Bank At Monte Carlo' was, in reality, a common (well, not THAT common) conman.

Whether Charles Deville Wells actually broke the bank by way of a con or fix seems unlikely - but he certainly made himself money by conning people out of their own cash. He sold off worthless rights to worthless inventions which he had patented.

When several of his conned investors become suspicious, Wells decided it was time to leave England for friendlier pastures - Monte Carlo sounded okay.

Wells turned up there in the 1880s and promptly managed to 'break the bank' three times in just three days.

It seems that Wells operated a system which involved just backing the number five in virtually any combination of bets possible. He would stake the maximum amounts allowed on the various bets and on each of the three occasions he won himself 90,000 francs (around £4500) - enough to put the particular table on which he was playing out of business.

Within three days of arriving in Monte Carlo with just £400 to his name, Wells had played it up to £40,000.

He became a massive celebrity. Publicity about him brought a massive surge in betting turnover for the casino; so it wasn't too depressed at his success.

Wells returned to England, where he lived a life of luxury in London until unhappy investors began to catch up with him again.

So off he set to Monte Carlo where, incredibly, lady luck smiled upon him again as number five once again turned up with surprising regularity. In just a few days at the beginning of November 1891 he

won another 250,000 francs.

At this time, songwriter Fred Gilbert spotted a newspaper hoarding with the headline, 'The Man Who Broke The Bank At Monte Carlo' and wrote the song which was made popular in music hall by singer Charles Coborn.

It couldn't last and it didn't.

On his third visit to Monte Carlo in January 1892 the rot set in. Not only Wells, but also the many who followed his system, began to suffer huge losses.

And back in London, the Fraud Squad had compiled a dossier on Mr Wells and his dubious investments.

In March 1893, Wells was convicted of obtaining £50,000 by false pretences and was sentenced to eight years penal servitude. He died a poor man.

Saving Scheme

Champion jockey Fred Archer was 'careful' with money - a favourite trick was to ask a bystander for the loan of a few coins to put in his waistband to make up his weight as he went to the scales - which he would then 'forget' to return.

Colour Scheme

William Douglas, Earl of March and Ruglen and fourth Duke of Queensbury, was better known as 'Old Q' and was reckoned to be one of his age's most outrageous roisterers.

On one occasion, shortly before a race, his jockey came to him to reveal he had been offered a large sum of money to pull his mount.

Old Q instructed the jockey to accept the bribe.

Later, as he helped to saddle the horse, Old Q suddenly announced: "I think I'll ride this myself." Removing the long coat he always wore, he revealed himself to be clad in his own racing colours.

To the amusement of his jockey, and the dismay of the would-be bribers, Old Q and his mount duly won the race.

On The Right Lines

Critic and jazz buff Benny Green tells an amusing cautionary gambling tale:

"My great uncle Jack made a comfortable living by placing bets on the course on behalf of owners whose presence at the bookies stand might have spoiled the odds.

One morning he boarded the train at Kings Cross bound for Doncaster with £500 to be wagered on the favourite nag of a certain racing peer.

On the train he met a well known jockey who had been sent to replace another who had broken his leg. The horse the jockey was to ride was the same one my great uncle was going to back.

My great uncle gave half the stake money to the jockey, kept half for himself, disembarked at Peterborough and came home, while the jockey went on to make sure the horse finished a respectable fifth."

The Big Stings

Perhaps the best known gambling 'sting' of all time, and still a model for the perfect coup, was the 1898 Trodmore Hunt affair - but two similar attempted frauds which took place nearly one hundred years after the original are less well documented.

In 1898, a newspaper called *The Sportsman* printed the card for the Trodmore Hunt meeting of 1 August and, subsequently, the results from the meeting - all 11 of which had been supplied to them by a plausible gentleman.

Suspicions were aroused when it became clear that no-one had ever heard of Trodmore. It transpired there was no such meeting - even though bookies had taken bets on the fictitious event when the details had appeared in The Sportsman.

The perpetrators of this con were never discovered.

Perhaps inspired by Trodmore, Colin McLean, a proof reader on the Sporting Life, came up with what seemed to him to be a fool-proof system to ensure that his dog bets were winners, in May 1966.

He simply altered the results from out of London tracks while he was checking the proofs of the paper, to make sure they corresponded with bets he'd placed.

Of course it was too blatant a scheme to survive for any length of time. He was finally rumbled and fined £100 for trying to obtain money by false pretences - although whether by then he had won more than £100 is not recorded!

In October 1974, another con-man pulled an inspired stroke, which would seem to have its origins in Trodmore.

He introduced himself at a Birmingham news agency, which supplied dog results from Cradley Heath, as a representative from the Sporting Life, then turned up at the track and, following the last race, duped the agency man by telling him not to bother to ring the Sporting Life as he, the conman, would phone the result over.

Unbeknown to the agency man, the conman had placed several hefty wagers on the last race for a trap four to beat trap five result; although that was not the correct outcome it was the one he rang through to the Sporting Life, declaring the forecast payment as £5.27.

The next morning the conman was paid out on one of his bets at a Putney, London betting shop - but he was unable to collect the rest of the £10 bets he had placed, and which should have netted him £527 a time, because, unbeknown to him, the size of his bets had meant that smaller bookies had 'hedged' them with larger firms. They had

had representatives at Cradley Heath who became alert to the bogus result, and quickly notified fellow betting shops.

However, the conman was never caught and the then Greyhound Editor of the Sporting Life, Archie Newhouse, was quoted as saying: "He must have been quite a conman. He even had what appeared to be Sporting Life notepaper!"

Chipping In

American gamblers were delighted to be offered an all-expenses paid holiday in London PLUS $1000 worth of chips to use at the Villa Casino in Bayswater.

It seemed too good to be true - and it was.

For once the gambling holiday makers got to London, in May 1969, they were systematically fleeced at the casino's dice-table, when the holiday organisers introduced crooked dice into the game.

Unfortunately for the six Americans who organised the sting, London police got wind of their ploy and raided the Villa Casino, discovering one of the Americans with five bent dice in his pocket.

The six were fined a total of £14,000.

Tote-al Joy

Four tote workers at Glasgow's Shawfield greyhound stadium thought they'd hit the jackpot with their new scheme - they printed winning tickets for themselves after the race was over!

However, they were rumbled when it was noticed that the number of tickets sold did not balance up with the figures recorded by the stadium's computer and the four were caught.

In November 1980 they were fined up to £50.

Bookies Carpeted

Belfast born Noel Furlong became an instant folk-hero on 12 March 1991 when his horse, Destriero, won the Trafalgar House Supreme Novices Hurdle at the Cheltenham Festival - winning him anything from £500,000 to £3 million, depending on which paper you read or which version of the story you believed.

But one thing was for sure - if his horse The Illiad had won the Champion Hurdle he could have collected up to £10 million. So huge were the double bets coupling Destriero, which won at 6-1, and The Illiad that the latter's odds tumbled from 12-1 to 11-2 before the 'off' of the Champion Hurdle.

Sadly for Furlong, who had won almost £2 million when The Illiad won The Ladbroke Hurdle in Ireland the previous January, the horse was never able to figure in the finish and was well down the field.

He wasn't saying just how much he'd won - but what wasn't disputed was the fact he was obliged to pay Customs and Excise

£500,000 on the eve of the Festival just to be allowed into the country.

The 53-year-old Dublin carpet dealer had earlier jumped £500,000 bail while facing charges relating to an alleged operation to evade tax on imported carpets. He had been due to appear at Kingston Crown Court in September 1985.

Although he would readily admit to the size of his first ever bet - half a crown on a 30-1 winner called Jackstandfast, placed when he was just 12 - Furlong would not be drawn on the exact amount he'd won on Destriero.

The Sporting Life quoted Furlong on 23 March as saying: "I stood to win nearly four million punts if The Illiad had landed the Champion Hurdle. I ended up winning a little less than a million on Destriero."

The sterling equivalent of a million punts at that time stood at £930,000.

However, the Sporting Life further quoted Furlong as saying: "I am 2.5 to 2.7 million punts up. It has been a super year."

It is now believed to be Furlong's ambition to pull off the first £10 million gambling coup.

Famous Plunges

Just like anglers are always telling stories of 'the one that got away', so every punter can tell the tale of the day he nearly cleaned up - but few of them can compete with Terry Ramsden's 'almost but not quite' yarn.

In August 1986, the owner and fearless backer, who had made a fortune operating in the Japanese financial markets, staked a £10,000 win treble on three runners trained by Alan Bailey.

Lack A Style won at Newmarket at 16-1, giving him £170,000 going on to Cry For The Clown, which won at 4-1.

Ramsden now stood to win a mere £8.5 million if his final selection, 9-1 shot Miss Milveagh, obliged. The filly led into the final furlong but was caught and beaten close home by Remain Free.

Ladbrokes's shareholders could breathe again.

Another famous Ramsden plunge saw him stake well over £100,000 on his horse Mr Snugfit in the 1986 Grand National - he would win over a million pounds if the horse won.

In the event, Ramsden missed out on the big payout but made a profit on his bet as Mr Snugfit finished strongly in fourth place.

Well Placed

Paul Cooper picked up a cool quarter of a million pounds with a tricast bet placed at Ladbrokes's Lower Richmond Road shop in May 1989.

Cooper laid out £16.50; Miss Daisy (20-1), Halvoya (25-1) and

Roysia Boy (33-1) duly came in first, second and third in the Dick Peacock Handicap at Thirsk - and made him a rich man.

Mmmmm Nice!

On the same day, a 26-year-old man from Dartford, Kent picked out five horses with names beginning with the letter 'M' as a tribute to his recently deceased sister, whose name also began with the same letter. For his £3.10 bet he won £22,900 from William Hill as Miss Daisy (20-1), My Lamb (9-1), Make Or Mar (5-1), Midfielder (12-1) and Must Be Magic (14-1) all won.

Mr Fixit

Arnold Rothstein, criminal, drug baron and gambler was widely believed to be the man who fixed the 1919 World Series - Baseball's equivalent of the FA Cup.

Someone, person or persons unknown, made available to no less than TEN Chicago White Sox players the small matter of $10,000 EACH to throw the game.

Rothstein, so the story went, had backed their opponents, Cincinnati, to win him $350,000.

Cincinnati duly won the match. The Chicago players' fix money was traced back to Rothstein.

There was a trial for conspiracy. Eight of the players were indicted. Rothstein was acquitted.

In 1925, Rothstein, by then into importing whisky and rum illegally, was implicated in one of the most astonishing decisions in World Championship boxing.

EVERYONE could see that Dave Slade had convincingly beaten Micky Walker in their World Welterweight Title clash.

Everyone, that is, apart from the two judges and the referee. They gave the fight to Walker. Rothstein, reported one paper, had cleaned up $60,000 on the controversial outcome.

Not so, hit back Rothstein - it was $80,000.

Rothstein died in ironic circumstances in 1928. The crime king had played in a big poker match and lost $30,000, which he paid in IOUs. Those he owed came looking for payment. For once, Rothstein was short of cash and couldn't - or wouldn't - pay.

Shortly afterwards, he was shot in the stomach. As he lay on his deathbed he was asked why he hadn't paid up.

The card game, said Rothstein, had been crooked.

Fat Chance

Brighton. 1790.

Fat, blubbery, but gambling mad Mr Bullock bet Lord Barrymore that he, Bullock, could beat young, pacey Barrymore in a foot race

over 100 yards.

"Rubbish," scoffed Barrymore, "name your stake."

"Very well," said Bullock, naming an amount, the exact value of which is lost in the mists of time, and demanding the right to name the course.

Barrymore agreed to this stipulation and the date for the race was decided upon.

News of the wager soon spread and spectators met in the street named for the event by Bullock.

The two men were asked whether they were ready to start, whereupon Bullock demanded his agreed start and set off into a 35 yard lead, down the narrowest street in Brighton - Black Lion Lane, where the walls on either side were down to 40 inches apart in places.

Barrymore caught Bullock up easily, but it was impossible for him to squeeze past and Bullock won the race.

Chapter XI

Sweet Charity

It had to be a con, surely - a letter from a punter wanting to GIVE BACK the £475 he had won in a bet.

I couldn't believe it when it happened in April 1990, there just HAD to be a scam to it.

If there was it has yet to be revealed!

The letter was from a gentleman in Glasgow calling himself just Mr M, who wrote:

"I won £475 in a bet with your company four years ago, involving two horses, but I now do not want the money and I am therefore returning it to you to do what you think/feel is best i.e put it back into horse racing or into a charity of your choice. An extra £25 has been added for the trouble to which this letter/money puts you i.e book keeping and money transfer. Total enclosed is £500 in Postal Orders."

Can you believe it? We couldn't, so we waited for a few weeks expecting some sort of follow up, but when none came we donated the money to a racing charity as requested.

Book-keeping

In October 1980, a client wrote to me with payment for a bet - which he had struck no less than twenty two years earlier!

Gilbert Claughton, from Cambridge, had struck a bet for the princely sum of one shilling and sixpence (7½p) on the Fixed- odds Pools on 8 November 1958.

"The reason for the delay was that the bill got lodged inside an old football annual and I forgot all about it until an advert for Hills in the Daily Mirror jogged my memory," explained the honest punter.

Slow Delivery

Gilbert was far more honest than Mathias Rararka from Nigeria, who wrote to me in 1987 claiming his winnings for a bet struck in February 1969. Investigations soon revealed that his winnings had been promptly despatched some eighteen years previously - so either Mathias was a conman or he should have a word with his postman!

Cash On Demand

All of which brings to mind allegations occasionally levelled at bookies that they con the public when it comes to 'sleeper' bets. Recently, someone came out with the incredible claim that bookies were making hundreds of thousands, if not millions of pounds, per year by holding on to cash which rightfully belonged to punters who hadn't collected their winnings.

This is almost too daft to be taken seriously, but requires an answer just in case there are some folk deluded enough to believe it.

Firstly, it must be pointed out that punters in betting shops are anonymous when they place their wagers. There is no requirement for them to leave any name or forwarding address so, in the unlikely event that they should forget to collect any winnings they may have, it would be very difficult to locate them if they are not regular punters in that particular shop.

If they ARE a regular in a shop then the Manager will invariably point out to them the fact that they have forgotten to collect their winnings.

It can happen, of course; a punter may leave a shop thinking he has lost and a Stewards Inquiry subsequently alters the result. He could lose his copy of his bet and forget what he's backed.

However, in the case of a lost receipt, bookies will happily pay out if the punter fills in a form and makes a copy of his bet.

Perhaps the client has a bet, then goes on holiday for a couple of weeks. No problem - his winnings will be there waiting for him on his return.

Even if he suddenly realises months later he has an unclaimed wager, dropping a line to the company concerned will result in full settlement of the bet once it has been confirmed that the bet was genuine.

Only a few months back William Hill's Customer Relations Dept spent a considerable amount of time locating a customer who was unaware he had a substantial amount of money to collect. And another wrote in, two years after placing a bet, to claim £200 which was quickly forwarded to him - even though he had lost his copy and had no idea in which shop he had originally placed the bet!

Another lady who had discovered a betting slip in a suit which hadn't been worn for over ten years was fully reimbursed by her bookie.

There are numerous instances of racecourse bookies paying out claims to punters who have left the races without collecting their winnings, or have forgotten which bookie they placed their bet with.

Despite all this, it must be pointed out that the onus really is on the customer to collect their winnings - there are some large players who may have a few pounds or pence to come back from a yankee or other combination bet who feel it would be beneath them to collect such a paltry amount. They will often tell the counter clerk: "Stick it in the charity box."

The amount of money never collected is very small - and it is ALWAYS available to the owner if a reasonable, verifiable claim is made.

By the way - when was the last time anyone drew attention to how much money credit bookies have to write off when punters default?

Another criticism sometimes levelled at bookies is that they have unjustifiably small payout limits - again, the onus is on the customer to be aware of just what the limits are in the particular shop in which he is betting, and if he is not happy about them to either bet elsewhere or to make sure that the stakes being used will not enable a winning bet to exceed the limits.

It is fair to say in general that the bigger the bookie the bigger the limit - although that was cold comfort to a certain Mr Edward Hodson from Wolverhampton who landed winning odds of 3,956,784-1 in February 1984 only to discover too late that his bookie (not one of the larger companies) had a maximum payout of £3000!

However, record-busting punters like Tony Tang (£217,708) of Catford, and a William Hill Stepney client (£227,812.50) had no complaints about the limits imposed in their betting shops when they landed their once in a lifetime wins.

Mug Punters

One of the worst examples of real gambling conmen can be unscrupulous tipsters who demand scandalous amounts of money from gullible punters in return for useless information.

I absolve from blame newspaper and other media tipsters who do a difficult job giving advice about potential winners to the best of their ability, who do it in an entirely open manner and who impose no financial obligation upon those who choose to take their advice.

No, I'm talking about the tipsters who advertise for mugs in the small ads columns of newspapers (although it must be pointed out that the reputable specialist papers do their best to monitor claims made by their advertisers and to weed out the crooks and conmen), or who approach people via direct mailing.

As my name is fairly well known in the racing business - I suppose I am on quite a few mailing lists - I had some unwelcome personal experience of a complete racing rip off when I opened my mail one day to discover a letter, addressed from Pudsey in Yorkshire, offering me GUARANTEED WINNERS for the small consideration of just £995.

The letter claimed to offer "the ultimate gamble" and instructed me to ring a telephone number on Saturday morning to discover the name of the unbeatable horse the service was tipping.

"As soon as this horse has won then you must post your

subscription by return. The service is known as 'Stable Jobs' and the charges are £5000 per year."

But this was clearly my lucky day, for the letter urged: "We will pass them on to you for just £995 per year."

I rang the number on Saturday morning and was given a tip (I use the word loosely) for a horse called Vestige, running in the 2.25 at Southwell, which, stressed the message, was as good as past the post already.

The message also reminded me to be ready to post off my subscription just as soon as the horse had won. I was advised to place my "maximum wager" (a fiver, in my case!) on this "good thing".

As inspired tips go, this one was about as difficult to pick out as Shergar would have been if he'd run against a field of pit ponies.

Virtually every newspaper selected the horse, it was widely expected to start hot favourite. In fact, it started at the restrictive odds of 2-7, at which price if I had placed £700 on it I would have stood to make a profit of a huge £200 - not to mention the £90 extra deductions had I placed it in a betting shop.

For my humble fiver I'd have been looking at winnings of about 80p!

This red-hot favourite was beaten out of sight, finishing third.

Clearly, the scheme being operated here (and still, doubtless in many other similar scams) involves naive or gullible punters being tipped a well fancied horse in the hope that it wins and persuades the punter to send off up to £1000 for a year's follow up tips.

In other cases the tipster will send different selections to different clients - thus guaranteeimg that some of them receive a winner.

And beware those tipsters who claim not to charge for their advice, but just ask you to send them the odds to a tenner (or even more) if the horse wins - a real no-risk scenario for the conman.

My free advice is to ignore these tipsters and their claims. They are almost invariably bogus - after all, if the tips were so good, why should the tipster share them with anyone else? Why not just back them himself, make a fortune and retire to a paradise island!

It is also worth taking the advice of the *Punters Protection Service*, set up to expose sham tipsters, who say: "The majority of these people are conmen whose brightly attractive letters and letterheads introduce themselves as top racing advisers selling unbeatable systems."

But what about tipsters who these days have harnessed new technology in their battle to win the battle with the bookies - can computers help you find winners? Or is this just another con?

I was sitting in my office, minding my own business, a while back when I received a phone call from a lady working for a Newcastle paper. Was I aware, she asked, that my company was about to be put out of business by a tipster with a computer?

"Well, no, actually," I told her, "would you care to elucidate?"

She told me of the exploits of one Cliff Goodwin, managing director of a company called KSB software, based in the North East.

Cliff, it seemed, had produced a computer programme called Master Tipper, which he was prepared to guarantee would give a 90% success rate.

Never being able to resist a challenge, I invited Mr Goodwin to set up his computer in one of William Hill's Newcastle branches and do his best - or worst, as the case may be. I'd even give him £100 of free bets to place on behalf of a local charity.

Sportingly, Mr Goodwin (who, it must be pointed out, is far from being a conman) agreed, so off I flew to Geordieland to test him out.

Not surprisingly, the local media turned out in force to film and record this confrontation.

Cliff was quietly confident, he told me over breakfast - but he was concerned enough for the well-being of the nation's bookies to promise that he'd keep the price of his programme high enough to deter all but the most fervent of winner seekers from buying it.

Came the big moment and Cliff's computer coughed out its selections for the afternoon's sport.

They were under orders for the first race containing one of Cliff's tips, the cameras rolled and a hushed atmosphere of expectation spread around the betting shop.

Cliff's horse, Absonant, was 11-8 favourite.

It ran out at the third hurdle.

Cliff was a little nonplussed at this. His next three selections fared somewhat better - well, comparatively - they all got around in one piece, anyway. But none of them won.

I went back to London.

Cliff went back to the drawing board.

If you really do reckon that computers can find winners then perhaps rather than spend large amounts of hard earned readies buying someone else's system why not invest less than £20 in a little machine called 'Race Track Computer' and available from mail order company, Innovations.

This machine, boasts its sellers, "uses a microchip processor to assess the entire field in a race, and rates the horses most likely to be first past the post."

Innovations further tempt would be purchasers by pointing out that "tests in the States have shown astounding results".

Innovations fail, though, to say whether the results are astoundingly good or, as seems more likely, astoundingly bad!

Perhaps computers can help - but even authors Tony Drapkin and Richard Forsyth, who wrote *The Punters Revenge*, which spends some 260 pages trying to show how computers can beat the bookies, are cautious enough to make only this low-key claim: "There are many kinds of gambling where a computer can give the modern punter a valuable edge - it is only a question of learning how to use it."

Talking of computers, one of the best known of them all is Ernie, the Premium Bond computer. Old Ernie's been around for some while now, and I think he may be showing his age. If you've got any Premium Bonds stashed away I suggest you dig them out and check the numbers each month to avoid being conned.

A while ago it was revealed, or admitted, that prize money has often been paid to the wrong people - but that the Government has no idea how often this might occur.

Commented a Government spokesman: "Such errors will generally only come to light when revealed by a third party. Any such cases which arise are very few in number and confined to very small prizes."

Well, before hearing that I'd always reckoned Bonds were a decent enough bet - at least you don't lose your stake money - but if they hand out the prizes willy-nilly perhaps they aren't quite such good value.

Pulling Strokes

I served my time as a betting shop manager - a job which ensures that at some time or other you come across local villains and small time conmen out to fleece not you personally, but your employer.

The problem is that so many people don't seem to have a problem morally with trying to part bookies from their cash - by fair means or foul, and they'll get up to strokes they would never even contemplate if dealing with, for example, a bank.

One of the most frequently attempted ruses in betting shops, and now often carried out by organised gangs, is the 'slow count' scam. This will almost invariably be attempted on a greyhound race or on a horse race sprint.

The punter, almost inevitably one you've never seen before, will approach the counter just before the 'off' of the race.

He will want to place a sizeable bet - perhaps £200 - on the favourite for the race, just as the dogs are going in the traps or the horses in the stalls.

He will hand his slip over the counter to the cashier but will then begin to laboriously dig around in his pickets for the money, which he will finally begin to count over in five pound notes, frequently miscounting and having to start again.

By this time the cashier is exasperated, there are probably people queuing up behind trying to place their bets, and the race has actually started.

Now is the key moment. The punter will be listening to the commentary or watching the TV screen intently - if the horse or dog he has backed jumps off in the lead he will complete the count, pay over all the money and be back in a trice for his winnings.

If he sees that his dog has missed the break or his horse has got away to a bad start he will suddenly announce that he didn't want the bet after all, grab back the cash and disappear.

With a large percentage of dog races won comfortably by the dog which hits the front first out of the traps - particularly if that dog is also favourite, this ploy has a good chance of working if it can be got away with.

These days, though, betting shop security is pretty tight and staff will have been warned about this trick and will be on the look out for it - so I can't recommend that you take it up as a profession.

A punter in the shop I used to manage in Harrow, Middlesex had a slightly less sophisticated con trick which he would frequently use.

A man of some talent in the noble art of boxing, and an infamous local personality not noted for his even temper, he was a keen punter. He loved to back a favourite and he loved to beat the odds.

Well aware of this gentleman's reputation, whenever he would ask me, "What price is the favourite?" - knowing full well that it was a 7-4 chance - I would invariably reply, "Oh, it's 2-1, Pat."

Now this exchange was really cloaked in a code which we both well understood.

In asking me what price the favourite was, he was really saying, 'You obviously don't expect ME to have to take that price, do you?; you'd be only too pleased to give me over the odds, wouldn't you?; you do want to be able to WALK home tonight, don't you?'

And I, cottoning on pretty quickly to the etiquette involved, was saying, 'Sure, Pat, whatever price you want, mate, would you like to come behind the counter and help yourself to the takings if it loses?'

In this manner, I ensured that I retained the loyalty of a chap who could prove a remarkably undesirable enemy - and many were the occasions on which the small over the odds concession paid off. Besides, it was cheaper than paying protection money!

Today, with cheques and bank-cards and direct-debit cards all usable in transactions with bookmakers there are cases of fraudulent use of these and the bookmakers and betting shops are also targets for those endeavouring to 'launder' crooked money or pass forged notes - staff are always on the look out for this particular con and many punters suffer a similar fate to the one who placed a bet with a forged £50 note in Cardiff.

His horse won, the punter duly received his winnings, minus £50 deductions to make up for the dodgy note - and he was then nicked by the local Constabulary.

Which is a fate which didn't befall the punter who placed a £200 bet with a manager friend of mine some while ago, but perhaps should have done.

This punter was a well known local worker for good causes in the area, who could often be seen in the High Street waving collection boxes under the noses of shoppers.

On one particular day he came into my friend's shop and passed him a note on which was written the message, 'Meet me out the back.'

My manager friend duly did so, only to be handed a betting slip and a huge bag full of copper and silver coin of the realm, adding up to a £200 stake.

Severely suspicious about the source of this stake money, but obviously unable to do anything about it, my friend put the bet on for the punter. Justice was done when the selection was beaten - although those people who had donated the money in good faith may have been somewhat surprised had anyone later told them that they had made a charity donation to a large bookmaking company!

Chapter XII

Dubious Derbies

1782: The third Derby may have been the first 'bent' one - it was won by Lord Egremont's Assassin, trained by a certain Mr Bird, who admitted on his death bed that he had twice won the Derby with FOUR-year-olds (the race is, of course, restricted to three-year-olds). However, he wouldn't reveal in which years this had happened, but he had also won it in 1804 with Hannibal, 1805 with Cardinal Beaufort, 1807 with Election and 1826 with Lapdog.

1812: Second favourite for the race Manuella was deliberately pulled by her jockey, Sam Chifney - who then staked £100 on her at 20-1 for the Oaks, in which she was ridden by a jockey called Pierce and won, beating the odds-on favourite Elizabeth. With Manuella out of the way, 7-1 shot Octavius won the Derby.

Manuella's owner, Mr Hewett, was unaware of the stroke Chifney had decided to pull and gambled so much on his filly to win the Derby that he was ruined despite her Oaks triumph.

1825: 7-4 favourite Middleton was the winner, despite a major attempt to prevent him doing so. The horse's lad was bribed to give the horse a bucket of water to drink shortly before the race, which he duly did. However, a four mile walk supervised by trainer Edwards did the trick, and despite still looking barrel-like at the post, Edwards's confidence that, "even with five gallons inside nothing would touch him" proved well founded and Lord Jersey's horse won by two lengths.

1827: Lord Jersey owned the winner Mameluke and the runner-up Glenartney - Mameluke a 9-1 chance, Glenartney the 5-1 favourite. It was widely rumoured that the noble Lord was better suited by the result than he would have been had the favourite obliged. Certainly the favourite's jockey, Edwards, had had a substantial wager on Mameluke and, despite the fact that with just two furlongs to run and with Glenartney seemingly going well within himself, Mameluke was able to cruise up alongside and go on to win by two lengths.

Mameluke was bought by prize fighter John Gully, who backed him heavily to win the St Leger and stood to win £40,000. But certain forces were determined that Mameluke should not win the Leger and it was curious that the odds remained steady no matter how heavily the horse was backed.

The starter was bribed successfully, with the result that - after a series of false starts - Mameluke was left well behind when the runners set off. Despite the best efforts of his jockey, Mameluke was still half a length down at the finish.

1832: It was said that all but four of the 22 jockeys who turned out for this Derby had been bribed to ensure the favourite, St Giles, owned by Yorkshire villain Robert Ridsdale, should win.

The horse duly won by a length and a half, following which it was alleged, probably correctly, that St Giles was, in fact, a four-year-old.

1840: Berwick on Tweed owner Mr Robertson failed to back his 50-1 Derby winner Little Wonder, although, strangely, his trainer, William Forth, seemed to have more faith in the horse and collected £18,000 when it won by half a length.

A possible explanation for Mr Forth's confidence was revealed when Sir John Astley wrote: "There is little doubt he was foaled a year earlier than his competitors."

During the race, when it became obvious that Little Wonder was about to beat the 9-4 favourite, Launcelot, into second place, the latter's jockey, Bill Scott, shouted across to Little Wonder's rider, the young W.MacDonald, "A thousand pounds for a pull!" - to which the youngster replied: "Too late, Mr Scott, too late."

1844: This was quite probably the single most crooked race in racing history. The so-called winner, Running Rein, turned out to be a four-year-old called Maccabeus.

Suspicions were voiced even before the race and a petition was presented to the Epsom Stewards, asking them to look into the situation. In a classic compromise, the Stewards announced they would allow the horse to run, but if he were to win, the stakes would be withheld, pending further inquiry.

'Running Rein' won by three lengths from Orlando, owned by Colonel Peel.

The Colonel demanded the stakes himself.

The owner of Running Rein/Maccabeus, Mr Wood, was nowhere to be found when the Stewards demanded to see him.

The outcome of the race went to law, with Mr Wood facing up against Colonel Peel. Realising he would have to produce his colt for investigation, Mr Wood, who had only acquired the horse in settlement of a debt owed to him by well-known rogue and gambler Goodman Levy, withdrew from the case.

Orlando was declared the winner of the Derby.

However, there were a number of other anomalies about this 29 runner race.

14-1 shot Leander broke a leg during the race. He was examined and discovered to be a four-year-old. His owners, German brothers named Lichtwald, were barred from the English turf, but not before declaring that the horse was certainly NOT four years old - he was in fact SIX!

Second favourite Ratan was pulled by his jockey, Sam Rogers, who was subsequently warned off.

The favourite, Ugly Buck, was deliberately impeded during the race to prevent him winning.

1846: There was no suggestion that he wasn't trying, but Bill Scott, owner of 16-1 shot Sir Tatton Sykes, would have won the race but for riding the horse whilst hopelessly drunk. He lost several lengths at the start arguing with the starter, before chasing after the field and ending up just a neck loser to Pyrrhus The First.

1853: Bookmaker and all round villain Harry Hill burnt his fingers severely when, believing that he had Derby favourite West Australia's jockey well and truly sewn up, he accepted huge wagers for the 6-4 shot.

Unfortunately for Mr Hill, a certain Colonel Anson, who had plunged on West Australia, got wind of the deal, sent for Frank Butler, the jockey, and made it plain to him how unpleasant life would become for him should he not ride the horse to the best of his ability.

In the end, Butler had to struggle to get West Australia home by a neck from Sittingbourne.

1855: Wild Dayrell, owned by country squire Francis Popham was the Derby favourite, but Mr Popham was concerned to discover that no matter how much money was plunged on his horse, the odds remained the same. He was suspicious - and rightly so.

His suspicions began to be confirmed when professional gambler George Hodgman was informed that Wild Dayrell would be 'settled' before the race.

Hodgman conveyed this information to the stable's connections, who increased their security measures.

Then Mr Popham himself was approached by someone who offered him £5000 not to run his horse. The offer was declined.

Later the van in which Wild Dayrell was due to travel to Epsom was interfered with, but again the stable's sources of information proved equal to the plot. They were alerted and instead of putting Wild Dayrell straight into the van they put in a bullock instead to try it out.

The van's wheels collapsed, it toppled over - and the hapless bullock inside broke a leg.

It became clear that those endeavouring to 'stop' Wild Dayrell had backed another leading fancy, Kingstown, owned by villain and bookie

Harry Hill. It was said they had fixed second favourite Lord of the Isles's jockey, Aldcroft, to ride his horse in a manner designed to assist Kingstown's chances.

In the event, with the crooks realising their efforts to stop Wild Dayrell had failed, they dug deep and placed huge saving bets on him, with the result that he started at Even money.

Wild Dayrell duly won by two lengths from Kingstown, 12-1, with Lord Of The Isles third.

Mr Popham won £10,000 but, exasperated by all the furore surrounding the race, declared that he never wished to own a Derby horse again.

1859: The Day family, so often in trouble for various misdemeanours, were involved in strange goings on again. 9-4 favourite Musjid, backed by his owner, Sir Joseph Hawley, to win him £75,000 duly obliged, but he must be ajudged a fortunate winner.

William Day rode and was part-owner of 2000 Guineas winner The Promised Land, which turned into the straight well clear and looking round for dangers.

Meanwhile Musjid's jockey, John Wells, had to evade the attentions of two other jockeys, who seemed determined to prevent him from getting a clear run.

Up front, The Promised Land was beginning to slow down, probably under persuasion from his jockey; Marionette, ridden by Sam Rogers, and Trumpeter, ridden by Alfred Day, joined issue.

It was said that Alfred Day stood to win £30,000 if Marionette was successful and he allegedly shouted over to Rogers that he should go on and win the race. At the same time Trumpeter was being held back.

But while these three tried to carve up the race between them, Musjid was making ground hand over fist and finally prevailed by half a length.

After the race it was confirmed that Alfred Day owned a share in Marionette and he was warned that he should dispose of that share or be barred from riding.

1863: An attempt to nobble favourite Lord Clifden was made when person or persons unknown dug holes in the gallops at Telscombe, near Lewes, where he was being prepared for the race, and filled them with flints. The trap was found in time.

Lord Clifden eventually finished second to Macaroni, a defeat which upset his jockey, George Fordham, greatly - so much so that when he heard a Mr Oldaker, Clerk of the Course at Harpenden, allege that his mount had been deliberately pulled, he threw him into a furze bush and administered a sound beating.

Contemporary reports suggest that whilst suffering this thrashing, Oldaker shouted: "Cheese it! Here sir, you cheese it!"

1864: A tendency for winner Blair Athol to display intermittent lameness baffled his trainer William I'Anson until a friend of his, Mr Colpitts, having his hair cut by a local barber, overheard a conversation revealing that Blair Athol's lad had been bribed to prevent the horse competing in the Derby and had taken to kicking him hard and regularly in the genitals!

The lad, discovered, suffered a similar fate himself before being sent on his way.

1880: The Duke of Westminster's Bend Or won the Derby, but Charles Brewer, owner of the runner-up Robert The Devil, objected on the grounds that Bend Or was in actual fact a horse called Tadcaster.

Brewer had been told by a stud-groom that when the Duke's Eaton stud handed a colt over to be trained by Robert Peck, it was actually Tadcaster rather than the genuine Bend Or.

The objection was overruled by the Epsom Stewards, although one of them, James Lowther, later declared he had seen additional evidence which made him doubt his decision had been correct.

1890: Surefoot was 95-40 ON for the Derby, but little did the watching crowd know that his JOCKEY had been got at! Liddiard, the rider, had a few weeks earlier been responsible for having several fellow jockeys 'stood down' for a period of a month.

Not best pleased at this betrayal of his own, those jockeys decided to get their own back. This they proceeded to do on Derby day itself, by firstly managing to fill Liddiard with gin prior to the event - not too difficult given his partiality to a drop or two.

Then, during the race, the jockeys made it their business to jostle and harass Liddiard and Surefoot, with the result that the best he could manage was fourth.

This plot was later revealed by jockey Jack Robinson, who rode the unplaced outsider Rathbeal in the race.

Chapter XIII

Er...Only Joking Lads!

Shortly after the shock resignation of Kenny Dalglish as Liverpool manager in early 1991, Scottish international Alan Hansen fooled the whole squad into believing he had taken over as their new boss.

He called the players together in the dressing room and laid down the law about how he intended to run the show.

Completely taken in, several senior players rushed off to the local bookies to bet on Hansen taking over - and his odds suddenly dropped from 7-2 to 7-4 favourite.

Later the same afternoon Hansen finally admitted he had pulled a fast one on his team-mates - and was shocked at their angry reaction as they suddenly realised they would be losing their stake money!

First Class Idea

A Brighton postman called Payne thought he'd come up with the perfect scheme to con his way to a massive pools win.

So the 26-year-old franked an envelope four days before the matches were due to be played and then filled in the results later on, sealing the envelope down and sending it off.

He was exposed when his 'winnings' were totalled up at £1.7 million and Littlewoods officials became suspicious.

Payne admitted fraud and was sentenced to 100 hours of community service in March 1991.

False Favourite?

Hard up Aussie pro runner John Dinan confessed to pulling a fast one when he won the Stawell Gift 120 metre handicap race in the early 1980s.

"Before the Stawell they'd made me an Even money favourite. During the parade of competitors I deliberately started to limp. We just told one person, in confidence of course, that my ankle had gone. The next day I was anything from 10-1 to 6-4. I won enough to pay all my debts and even bought a car."

Smile Please!

The Times reported on a real gambling con which was perpetrated in America on crooked politicians, who were prepared to take bribes to assist with the setting up of a casino.

Reported the paper in April 1991:

"Shot from concealed cameras, the films are grainy, the soundtracks poor, but Arizona's television stations have screened them night after night to record audience figures. Don Kenney, Republican chairman of Arizona's house judiciary committee, is shown stuffing a $55,000 (£31,500) bribe into a nylon gym bag and joking, 'Are you sure there are no hidden cameras?'

Carolyn Walker, Democratic whip in the Arizona Senate, remarks that 'we all have our price' as she collects part of her $25,800 bribe. 'I'm trying to position myself so that I can live the good life and have more money...I want to die rich.'

Bobby Raymond, a Democratic Legislator, sells his vote for $12,105. Sue Laybe, another Democrat, accepts and deftly counts out $10,000 in $100 bills. In each case the politicians were confiding in a loudly dressed man, dripping with jewellery, who called himself J.Anthony Vincent and purported to be a wealthy Las Vegas casino operator with mob connections.

In each case their confidence was misplaced. 'Vincent' was Joseph Stedino, a one time Las Vegas television show host with a string of convictions and a gaming background, being paid $3,500 a month by the Phoenix police chief. Over 16 months, operating from a plush Phoenix office provided by the police, Mr Stedino lined up Arizona's politicians to legalise gambling, saying he wanted to open a casino in the State. He handed out more than $350,000 in bribes as part of a $1 million 'sting', dubbed 'Operation Desert Shame'."

Some You Win, Some You Lose

When gambler Parmjit Singh of New York began to boast of the fortune he had won on the horses, his wife saw an opportunity to con him.

Singh received a phone call telling him his wife had been kidnapped by a gang and that a ransom of $35,000 was being demanded.

Singh had not, in fact, won anything on the horses - it was an empty boast, so he called in the Police to hunt for his wife.

They soon found her - at her lover's home, where she and the lover, believing the unfortunate Singh's boast, had dreamed up the kidnap ruse to relieve him of his winnings.

She ended up facing extortion charges and Singh ended up with no money and no wife.

An Ace Plan

In order to deter the Brazilian public from gambling, the importation of playing cards into the country was at one time banned - all they could use were the inferior, easily doctored, local version.

Consequently, there was (and may well still be) a flourishing black market trade in good quality cards.

One Brazilian exploited this fact with a simple, yet brilliant stroke which made him a rich man.

The Brazilian ordered a massive quantity of playing cards from an American manufacturer; with one stipulation - they must have the Ace of Spades removed from every pack.

Meanwhile, he arranged that all the Aces of Spades should be imported in one job lot. They passed through customs without a hitch - after all, what use was a consignment of Aces?

As expected by the Brazilian, his huge order of Ace-less packs hit problems at customs, where they were confiscated.

Discovering the packs to be without Aces the customs decided to auction them off.

The Brazilian duly bought the whole lot at a knock down price, reinserted the Aces and proceeded to sell them off at a vastly inflated price!

That's Alright Then

Punters were astonished at the announcement by Stewards who quizzed Irish trainer Paddy Mullins, following the 20-1 big race win of a horse of his which had recently been beaten at odds-on in a two horse race. The Stewards announced they had accepted Mullins's explanation that he had no explanation!

Straight Man

The legendary Fred Archer was an ultra honest man. In his book *Men And Horses I Have Known*, fellow jockey and trainer George Lambton tells of an occasion at Windsor when a trainer called Golding asked Archer, "if he would ride a brute of a horse called Westwood."

Archer answered that he would but warned Golding: "I am going to have £500 on Domino."

Lambton recalls Golding saying this would not matter as Westwood had no chance anyway.

But, says Lambton, "In the race, Archer, riding like a demon, got up and beat Domino by a neck, after having twice nearly gone into the river in two false starts."

Pick A Card

Picture postcards of horses had an unexpected value in Florida in the mid 1920s.

Hialeah racecourse opened there in 1925, although betting was illegal. To get around this problem, picture postcards of the runners were sold; if you had one showing the winner of a race the course would purchase it from you - at an appropriate premium.

Each-Way Bet

It was a case of 'heads you lose, tails we win' at Oakley point-to-point meeting in Northamptonshire in June 1989, where, following a dead heat for first place in one race, the Tote returned stakes to those who had backed either winner - and kept the rest of the pool.

Persse Strings

Desperate to prevent anyone else discovering what was going on when a horse was being especially prepared to land a gamble, betting trainer Atty Persse would lock his stable lads into their sleeping quarters every night for fear they might spill the beans.

Running Ringers

Three years hard labour was the final reward received by Peter Barrie when he was finally convicted of running ringers.

In the autumn of 1919, he managed to substitute useful three-year-old Jazz for useless two-year-old Coat Of Mail in the Faceby Plate at Stockton - despite the fact the two looked completely dissimilar.

Barrie owned horses with trainer Walter Hopkins, who owned the sickly Coat Of Mail, which Barrie entered for the Faceby Plate under an assumed name.

Hopkins had meanwhile purchased Jazz for £800, and it was the brown colt Jazz which lined up for the race instead of the bay Coat Of Mail, The horse promptly romped home - causing something of a sensation as he was backed from 20-1 down to 5-2 favourite.

Barrie was said to have won at least £3000 by backing the horse.

The racing press drew attention to the race, but Barrie seemed to have got away with it. He then set about pulling off another coup - this time 'inventing' a non-existent horse which he entered for a poor Cheltenham event, actually starting a useful hurdler, Shining More.

The invented horse, Silver Badge, had been described as a brown mare - Shining More was a bay with a white blaze and hind fetlock - so Barrie dyed Shining More!

Once again the switch worked, Shining More won by 6 lengths at 10-1 - Barrie won £7000.

Once again the media began to ask awkward questions.

The third time Barrie, a failed motor car dealer, attempted a coup it went wrong; Golden Plate, a three-year-old put in with two-year-olds, being soundly beaten by them in a race at Chester.

By now people were talking and the police had become involved, Barrie and a number of fellow schemers were arrested, charged and convicted.

The lightest moment during the case against Barrie occurred when a magistrate asked him: "What is your idea of a good thing in racing,

Mr Barrie?"
"A useful three-year-old in a moderate two-year-old race," he replied.

Trusted Customer

It is said that 1930's owner Dorothy Paget, although eccentric enough to sleep all day and work by night, was so honest and straight that her bookmaker would allow her to back her horses in the evening, even though they had run earlier that day - trusting her not to have discovered the results.

Out Of Luck

In 1947, when jockey Gordon Richards was at the height of his powers, a punter thought he'd come up with a surefire way of making his betting pay.

He made a standing order bet with his bookmaker that he wanted to back Gordon's best mount of the day to win him £1000.

All went well, with many more winners than losers, until one fateful day in June when Gordon rode 20-1 ON shot Glendower in a two horse race - which meant the punter was investing £20,000 to win £1000.

Glendower whipped around at the start of the race and unseated Gordon, leaving his solitary opponent, Markwell, to win as he liked.

Listening In

Security men had to be introduced to the Stewards Room at Towcester racecourse a couple of years ago, after it was revealed that a number of punters had taken to pressing their ears against the rickety door of the room in order to get advance information on the outcome of Stewards' Inquiries.

Bear-Brained Scheme

The 'bear-faced' cheek of racegoer Colin Eastick, 18, caused chaos as favourite Swift Fox challenged rival Where's The Limo in the final stages of Sunderland stadium's Mailcom Northern Puppy Derby, in November 1990.

Twelve hundred fans were enthralled as the two dogs battled it out with 30 metres to run - only for Eastick to suddenly hurl a teddy-bear onto the track. It hit Swift Fox, looking as though he was just about to take the lead.

'Panda-monium' broke out as racegoers chased the culprit, who was trying to escape through the main gate of the stadium to a waiting car. He was finally caught by two plain clothes policemen, and a police spokesman commented: "If we hadn't taken him away the crowd might have lynched him."

Eastick reportedly said: "I did it because I think it is cruel to the dogs." Many racegoers believed there may have been a more sinister motive to his actions.

Eastick was later fined £100 by Sunderland magistrates, with £82 costs, a sentence which caused racing pundit John McCririck to comment: "Such oddly incomprehensible leniency will only encourage a rash of similar 'jests'."

Missing The Jackpot

Giosue Zanca decided to con his best pal, Francesco Sambagini, when, after many years of filling in a joint entry for the football pools, they finally won.

Zanca, who had filled in the coupon when they won in March 1991, told Sambagini that he intended to keep all the winnings.

Sambagini shot Zanca dead.

It turned out they had only won £170!

The Worst Nightmare

Australian publican Walter Craig thought he had come up with a dream coup when in his slumbers he 'saw' his own horse, Nimblefoot, a little considered outsider, passing the post first in the prestigious Melbourne Cup.

One oddity of the dream was the fact that Nimblefoot's jockey appeared to be wearing a black armband - but Craig assumed it was a symbol of his bookmaker's despair at having to pay him out, so he rushed off to place a bet on the horse. His local bookie, a sceptical type not given to believing in dream winners, gladly offered a bet of £10,000 to a cigar (worth about 25p), which Craig gladly accepted.

Come Melbourne Cup day, Nimblefoot duly stormed home in first place - and, what's more, the jockey was wearing a black arm-band.

Because Craig had died the day before.

There was another dream ending to the race in 1931 when hundreds of Melbournites rang local papers with stories of having dreamed that a horse with a white nose would win the race - and a horse CALLED White Nose won!

Reverse Forecast

Florida greyhound punter Alfred Alchediak assumed he had cracked it with his first, second and third forecast bet on a race at Tampa greyhound track in 1988. He reckoned he stood to win £750 after K's Broadway finished first, Ari Cannon second and Oshkosk Zest third.

But the track stewards disqualified third placed Oshkosh Zest - because he crossed the finishing line backwards!

The dog had tripped on the heels of the runner-up as they came to the line and gone over in a back-flip.

After the stewards disqualified the dog, Alchediak set out on a three-year battle to have the dog reinstated - he went to court no less than five times, only to have his case finally rejected.

Had the race taken place in the UK, Mr Alchediak would almost certainly have won his bet - over here the important factor is where the dog's nose crosses the line and it doesn't much matter which way up he is at the time, providing he hasn't hampered other runners.

Playing With Fire

Jockeys often bear the brunt of 'fix' allegations, but in Athens in July 1990 it was the jockeys who accused the officials at the track of being involved in the rigging of races - and so upset did they become about the scandal, they set fire to the Phaleron Delta track!

Several jockeys were later charged with arson.

Low Down Crooks

As early as the beginning of the eighteenth century, card sharpers were making a healthy living out of fleecing naive opponents - particularly in Bath, where the card tables flourished.

One visitor to the tables there, the Earl of Chesterfield, revealed in a letter to his son that he actually enjoyed playing with the sharpers. "If I play with sharpers and win, I am sure to be paid, but if I win off gentlemen, they frequently behave so genteelly that I get nothing but words and polite apologies for my money."

The good Earl was not a great player, however, as was revealed by Horace Walpole who once wrote of a nobleman who was at Bath that he "would be in prison if his creditors did not occasionally release him to play and cheat my Lord Chesterfield, as the only chance they have of recovering their money".

Not all card players were as tolerant of the cheating sharpers as the Earl - one discovered cheat, nicknamed 'The Baron', was simply thrown out of the second floor window of the room in which his dubious methods were discovered. He was later discovered bemoaning his fate by a friend to whom he complained bitterly and demanded, "What should I do?"

The friend, clearly of a more practical bent than his cheating acquaintance, merely commented: "Do? Why, it's a plain case - as long as you live, never play so high again!"

A card sharper called Newman was caught in the act by an opponent who promptly snatched a fork which he plunged through the back of Newman's hand, skewering it to the card table.

The player told Newman: "Sir, if you have not a card hidden under that hand, I apologise."

Wheeling And Dealing

Probably the most successful roulette player ever to frequent the Monte Carlo casino was a gentleman called William Darnborough, an American who eventually settled in England.

Between 1904 and 1911 it was estimated he won a total of £83,000.

A contemporary, the Hon S.R.Beresford, who wrote about him some while later, commented: "He undoubtedly broke all records for continuous gain, for every shilling of his money was won upon the numbers at roulette."

Darnborough himself, who was deeply steeped in the world of gambling before arriving at Monte Carlo, never revealed the secret of his success and kept himself very much to himself - however two theories gained supporters at the time.

The first was that he was actually in league with the casino and his success was merely a massive publicity stunt designed to attract gullible punters into the casino, believing that they, too, could become great winners.

The second was that he had perfected a means of conning the casino by taking advantage with a unique system.

The latter was explained by a writer named C.N.Williamson in a 1913 magazine article.

"Everyone wondered how he did it - what was the secret? His play was on numbers, but seemed to vary from time to time, often skipping from one side of the wheel to the other. No-one could understand what he was doing.

It was declared, by those who claimed to have inside information, that the clever American had worked his system with the aid of an assistant who was always with him at the tables.

The American used to stand while he played, with one shoulder towards the wheel, and it was said that his assistant, standing at the opposite side of the table, keenly watching the wheel, signalled to the player at the last instant into which quarter of the cylinder the ball seemed likely to fall."

Whether this story is true or not, it is not impossible. Many thought it the only way to account for such a long and persistent run of luck with a system based on numbers.

The Last Word

The ultimate warning against the dangers of being conned over a gamble must surely be the one delivered by American writer Damon Runyan in one of his short stories (Constable & Co Ltd). He was describing a conversation in which a father was speaking to his would-be professional gambler son:

"No matter how far you travel, or how smart you get, always remember this: someday a guy is going to come up to you and show you a nice, brand new deck of cards on which the seal is never broken, and this guy is going to offer to bet you that the Jack of Spades will jump out of the deck and squirt cider in you ear. Son, do not bet him - for as sure as you do, you are going to get an ear full of cider."

Postscript

A golf compiler working for William Hill told me that a friend of his had made a very lucrative living by asking bookmakers in the Midlands to quote him odds about a hole in one being scored in major tournaments and then plunging on if the gullible bookie offered anything longer than about 5-1.

The true odds are round about Even money!

This chap in the Midlands was being quoted odds of 33-1 and bigger - no wonder he cleaned up! In 1990 holes in one were scored in 30 of the top 38 events, by the time of the 1991 Open Championship, 20 holes in one had been scored in 21 European Tour events.

In the 1991 British Open William Hill offered 4-5 about a hole in one being scored - it was done in the very first round. Another bookie, rather less well up in golf betting, offered the suicidal odds of 100-1 - and was left with a large hole in his pocket.

The basis of calculating the likelihood, was told by a former odds compiler, Tommy Graham was that the chances of any one shot being hit by a half-way decent golfer at a par three hole turning into a hole in one were 1000-1. It is then a simple matter of dividing the number of shots taken into one thousand to get the approximate odds. But don't forget that once there is an incentive offered for scoring a hole in one rather than playing a straightforward shot.

About ten years ago there was a fashion amongst sponsors of golf tournaments for offering incentive prizes like apartments or Rolls Royces for anyone scoring a hole in one - they were almost inevitably won.

I remember, some years back, William Hill offering odds about Tony Jacklin being able to score a hole in one in four attempts on behalf of the winners of a prize competition. If he succeeded he would win £400,000 for the prize winners.

He came within several inches of taking the money and giving Hill's Director Roy Sutterlin, who had authorised the bet, a nasty scare.

And - as previously mentioned, the hole in one issue came very much to the fore following the 1991 British Open when it transpired that a very shrewd punter or punters had been able to persuade smaller bookies to lay some fancy odds about a hole in one being scored during the event.

Whereas the large companies were unwilling to offer anything better than Evens some lesser fry had laid bets at odds of up to 100-1 and when it was done they were not happy. In fact they were crying 'con' and announcing that they would be referring bets to the Sporting Life.

More than that - if the Life refused to agree with them, the bookies, then the bookies would change their rules and not accept the Life ruling.

This was clearly outrageous behaviour by the bookies who had offered the odds of their own free will and happily accepted the wagers - would they have been shouting 'foul' and demanding to pay the punters back if the bets had been lost?

Midlands bookmaker Arthur Whitaker took - £50 bets at 100-1; Liverpool's Grandstand Racing took two £50 bets at 16-1; Mike Langley of Southport also laid 16-1; Peter Smith of Cannock took £200 at 7-1.

Many other, similar bets were reported in the trade press and Brian Marchbank's ace meant that they were all winning bets.

Dave Buckley, an independent bookie in South Wirral, revealed that he had laid 33-1 to two £20 bets - he paid up with good grace; "We got our fingers burnt but you have to learn by your mistakes" he was reported as saying.

The *Sporting Life* made a front page ruling: "Unless a bookmaker who has laid over generous odds about a hole in one has a clear and unambiguous rule giving him the right to void or amend the bet for good reason, he has no option except to pay up."

On Tuesday, July 30, 1991, the Life reported that Arthur Whitaker had refused to pay £15,000 to two punters who had taken three £50 bets at odds of 100-1 against a hole in one being achieved at three golf tournaments.

The two, in their twenties, claimed to have visited a "substantial area" of Britain seeking out attractive odds against aces. "It was a gamble that could have gone wrong" said one, "There was no guarantee there would be a hole in one."

"Most layers are honourable but others are moaning and groaning, looking for a reason not to pay."

But the bookies crying foul and offering to settle at vastly reduced 'realistic odds' were even attacked by their own National Association of Bookmakers Director, Don Butler, commented, "They have not done their homework and will have to pay."

It is likely to be some while before the same 'stroke' can be pulled again

BIBLIOGRAPHY

A Race Apart	Reg Green	*Hodder-Stoughton*
Complete Guide To Gambling	John Scarne	*U.S.A.*
Druids Lodge Confederacy	Paul Mathieu	*J.A.Allen 1990*
Eccentric Gamblers	J.A.Maxtone Graham	*Mowbrays 1975*
Gamblers Of Yesteryear	Russell.T.Barnhart	*GBC Press 1983*
Gambling	Alan Wykes	*Aldus 1964*
Infamous Occasions	John Welcome	*Michael Joseph 1980*
J.F.B.	Noel Fairfax-Blakeborough	*J.A.Allen 1978*
Light Come, Light Go	Ralph Nevill	*MacMillan 1909*
Men And Horses I Have Known	George Lambton	*J.A.Allen*
No Secret So Close	Bruce Hobbs	
Racetrack Ring-ins & Rorts	Cecil Cripps	*Vetsport 1989*
Rogues Go Racing	W.Bebbington	*Good & Betts 1939*
Soccer In The Dock	Simon Inglis	*Collins Willow 1985*
Taken For A Ride	Brian Radford	*1982*
The Education Of A Poker Player	Herbert.O.Yardley	*Oldcastle*
The Encyclopaedia Of Gambling	Carl Sifakis	*Facts On File 1990*
The History Of The Derby Stakes	Roger Mortimer	*1962*
The Punters' Revenge	Tony Drapkin/	*Chapman &*
	Richard Forsyth	*Hall/Methuen*
The Turf Expositor	C.F.Brown	*1829*
The Victorian Underworld	Kellow Chesney	*PBS 1970*